BEST PRACTICES FOR
Investment Committees

Rocco DiBruno,
AIFA™ Accredited Investment Fiduciary Analyst

WILEY

John Wiley & Sons, Inc.

Copyright © 2006 by Rocco DiBruno

Published by John Wiley & Sons, Inc., Hoboken, New Jersey
Published simultaneously in Canada

No part of this publication may be reproduced, stored in a retrieval system, or
transmitted in any form or by any means, electronic, mechanical, photocopying,
recording, scanning, or otherwise, except as permitted under Section 107 or 108 of the
1976 United States Copyright Act, without either the prior written permission of the
Publisher, or authorization through payment of the appropriate per-copy fee to the
Copyright Clearance Center, 222 Rosewood Drive, Danvers, MA 01923, (978) 750-8400,
fax (978) 646-8600, or on the web at www.copyright.com. Requests to the Publisher for
permission should be addressed to the Permissions Department, John Wiley & Sons,
Inc., 111 River Street, Hoboken, NJ 07030, (201) 748-6011, fax (201) 748-6008, or
online at www.wiley.com/go/permissions.

Limit of Liability/Disclaimer of Warranty: While the publisher and author have used
their best efforts in preparing this book, they make no representations or warranties with
the respect to the accuracy or completeness of the contents of this book and specifically
disclaim any implied warranties of merchantability or fitness for a particular purpose. No
warranty may be created or extended by sales representatives or written sales materials.
The advice and strategies contained herein may not be suitable for your situation. You
should consult with a professional where appropriate. Neither the publisher nor the
author shall be liable for damages arising herefrom.

For general information about our other products and services, please contact our
Customer Care Department within the United States at (800) 762-2974, outside the
United States at (317) 572-3993 or fax (317) 572-4002.

Wiley publishes in a variety of print and electronic formats and by print-on-demand.
Some material included with standard print versions of this book may not be
included in e-books or in print-on-demand. If this book refers to media such as a CD or
DVD that is not included in the version you purchased, you may download this material
at http://booksupport.wiley.com. For more information about Wiley products, visit
www.wiley.com.

ISBN 978-1-592-80309-5

Printed in the United States of America

10 9 8 7 6 5

Contents

Foreword

Investment risk is a term with which nearly everyone has, at least, some familiarity—an understanding painfully reinforced by the recent dot.com crash and bear market. Fiduciary risk, on the other hand, is a topic most people would struggle to define.

Quite simply, *fiduciary risk* is defined as the degree of uncertainty associated with a fiduciary's management of investment decisions.

In the case of a 401(k) plan, the tipping point for fiduciary risk is directly related to the conduct of the plan's investment committee. If the committee puts together a lousy selection of mutual funds and/or fails to control investment expenses, no amount of participant education is going to make up the shortfalls in the participant balances.

By law, the investment committee must demonstrate that its investment decisions are procedurally prudent—they will be measured against a prudent expert standard. What constitutes a prudent process? Who should be involved? How should the committee be governed? How much reliance should the committee place on outside "consultants"?

All relevant questions will be answered in this timely text.

The management of an investment committee is no different from the management or supervision of any other business enterprise. It does not require committee members who have extensive experience in securities analysis or portfolio management; it does require selecting members who have an interest in understanding the basics of capital markets.

It requires selection of a team that has a sincere commitment and courage to develop a consensus formulation of goals and objectives with fellow committee members, the discipline to develop long-term investment policies, and the patience to evaluate events calmly in the context of long-term trends. It requires putting together a committee that has the ability to get the right things done—otherwise known as effective management. Prudent procedures, such as the ones outlined in this book, facilitate effective management by distinguishing the important tasks of the investment committee from the unimportant.

All the best,

Donald B. Trone,
Strategic Ethos, CEO (Chief Ethos Officer)

Introduction

For many, the term investment committee conjures images of a group of seasoned financial experts who are highly qualified and skilled in managing an investment portfolio. In reality, most individuals who sit on a 401(k) investment committee are likely to have little or no experience in managing an investment portfolio. In this post-Enron, and ever increasing litigious environment, I feel compelled to write a simple guidebook, *Best Practices for Investment Committees,* that will provide a clear and concise explanation of how to successfully structure an investment committee.

This book is part of an ongoing series offered by Thornburg Investment Management to provide education and insight to financial advisors and plan sponsors in the area of fiduciary responsibility for qualified retirement plans, specifically 401(k) plans. The first installment in the series, *Understanding ERISA—A Compact Guide to the Landmark Act,* by Ken Ziesenheim, explains the Employee Retirement Income Security Act (ERISA), including the standards that govern fiduciary conduct of 401(k) plan sponsors and providers. It focuses on the fact that any person(s) who exercises any discretionary authority or control in management or administration of the plan or its assets is indeed a fiduciary. The book outlines the duties and fiduciary responsibilities under ERISA and shows how following a prudent process can mitigate fiduciary exposure.

A second book, entitled *How to Write an Investment Policy Statement*, by Jack Gardner, details the steps that should be taken in preparing an investment policy statement (IPS)—a written document outlining the process for a plan's investment-related decision making. The purpose of the IPS is to provide a formal description of a plan's goals and objectives as well as to serve as an objective framework for an investment committee to use in making investment decisions that are reflective of and in keeping with the plan's strategic vision for investing.

Now this third book in the Thornburg series, *Best Practices for Investment Committees*, guides committee members through the next step—how to execute and implement the plan's investment policy. The book discusses the benefits of having an investment committee and examines the roles and responsibilities of committee members. Though the book was written primarily for 401(k) plans, many of the concepts can be applied to trustees and individuals who sit on the board of an endowment, foundation, or public retirement plan. Because investment committees are made up of individuals who may have different ideas and levels of experience in managing money, the concepts in this book, along with implementation of the investment policy statement, can help an investment committee develop a disciplined, yet practicable decision-making process. Following the suggestions and ideas in *Best Practices for Investment Committees* can serve as a valuable risk management tool against potential fiduciary liability.

About the Author

Rocco DiBruno, AIFA® (Accredited Investment Fiduciary Analyst), is the director of the Retirement Group at Thornburg Investment Management and the investment advisor for Thornburg mutual funds. He is responsible for investment-only mutual fund sales and marketing of the company's value-added programs to plan service providers and financial advisors. Prior to joining Thornburg in 2003, Rocco was a vice president and regional sales manager responsible for employer-sponsored retirement plan sales and marketing at Merrill Lynch.

Rocco has over 25 years experience working with financial advisors and plan sponsors in retirement plan sales, consulting, marketing, and product development. He is also a frequent industry speaker on retirement industry trends and fiduciary governance.

Rocco holds the Accredited Investment Fiduciary Analyst™ (AIFA) designation from The Center for Fiduciary Studies. He is a graduate of Temple University in Philadelphia, PA.

The author's background gives him the opportunity to observe the activities of investment committees, ranging from the smallest to the largest, and even those entrusted with modest resources. In addition, Rocco shares his experience to articulate a set of best practices that should be adopted by 401(k) investment committees or anyone entrusted with making investment decisions.

BEST PRACTICES FOR

Investment Committees

Chapter 1

WHY YOU NEED A 401(k) INVESTMENT COMMITTEE

S tudies show that many of today's 401(k) plans do not offer a fully diversified menu of investment choices. "Nearly two-thirds of 401(k) plans aren't offering enough choices and lack the right types of funds needed to create a diversified portfolio suited to each worker's risk tolerance". [1]

One of the common misconceptions in the 401(k) retirement market is that when the plan participants are responsible for making their own investment decisions (also commonly referred to as *participant directed plan*), then the plan sponsor is free from liability relative to the investment options. This is a complete fallacy. Under the Employee Retirement Income Security Act (ERISA), 401(k) plan sponsors are accountable for providing plan participants with an array of appropriate investment options to allow the participants to properly diversify and avoid the risk of large losses. However, the plan sponsor has a fiduciary obligation to monitor these investment options on an ongoing basis to ensure they continue to be prudent and appropriate for use.

---

[1] *Wall Street Journal* (2/15/05). Data were based on a study conducted by finance professors at New York University and Fordham University, which analyzed 417 plans using data from Moody's Investors Services and the University of Chicago Center for Research in Security Prices.

A best practice for company sponsors of 401(k) retirement plans is to form an investment committee to participate in the governance of the plan and to oversee the plan's investment options. Small-plan sponsors typically argue against having investment committees, especially for smaller plans, and suggest that it is too time consuming. "My partners and I review the funds as need-be," says one small-plan sponsor. Sponsors of 401(k) plans need to understand that under ERISA they are fiduciaries and as such are personally liable for their actions. Having such a casual approach to the very important process of monitoring the appropriateness of the investment options being provided to the participants leaves them fully exposed to lawsuits. In today's environment, the best way for plan sponsors to manage their fiduciary liability is to develop, follow and document a prudent investment process.

Establishing a Benefits Committee

Advancements in technology and productivity have given us access to products and services that previously were thought to be unavailable or unaffordable. For one, it wasn't that long ago that automobile safety features like antilock brakes and airbags were available only in high-end luxury cars like Mercedes-Benz or Lexus. Currently they are standard features whether you are driving a car that costs $70,000 or $17,000. There are many examples of products and services that originate up market and eventually trickle down to all consumers. Most large pension and 401(k) plan sponsors, as well as nonprofit and government plans, use an investment committee to oversee the investment management process. The reason is simple: protect the plan against potential or unforeseen liability. In light of poor investment performance, lack of understanding of plan fees and revenue sharing arrangements, mutual fund scandals, and the recent wave of new investment products (lifecycle and lifestyle funds, managed accounts), the need for plans of all sizes to form a benefits committee or separate investment committee is becoming an important factor in the management of 401(k) plans. Regardless of whether your company has a plan with $1 million or $100 million in assets, ERISA standards are nondiscriminatory and are applied equally.

Let's take a closer look. ERISA requires that all plans have a plan administrator and named fiduciary who are responsible for the operation and administration of the plans. A common practice for ERISA covered plans is the establishment of a benefits committee to serve as the plan administrator and named fiduciary, because many functions of the benefits committee are fiduciary in nature and must be carried out in the best interests of plan participants and beneficiaries. (AON). To comply with their obligations, fiduciaries must exercise the care of a prudent person who is familiar with all aspects of the plan and investment issues. Although benefits committees have ultimate responsibility, they often delegate some of their fiduciary duties by forming an investment committees or employing outside service providers.

The investment committee is responsible for managing the investment process for the plan, whereas the benefits committee is charged with much broader responsibilities of administering the plan. The benefits committee's responsibilities are the non-investment related issues such as plan design, administration issues, and employee communications.

In this highly charged environment of corporate governance, regulatory scrutiny, and fiduciary liability exposure, the creation of a separate investment committee (whose responsibility is limited to reviewing the investments in the companey's 401 (k) plan), is a sound risk management strategy for plans of all sizes.

The Role of the Investment Committee

The scope of fiduciary responsibility for investment committees is much wider than generally recognized because the ERISA definition of fiduciary is so broad. Named fiduciaries are those listed in the plan documents as having responsibility for plan management. Persons who are delegated duties by named fiduciaries are also considered to be named fiduciaries and, therefore, assume the responsibilities and liabilities that go along with that obligation.

The investment committee is charged with establishing a prudent process by which retirement plan vendors, investment products offered (whether separate accounts or mutual funds), and related expenses are analyzed and monitored on a regular and consistent basis. However, it is important to keep in mind that committee members oversee the management of the retirement plan, but do not manage it themselves. In general, the investment committee has the following responsibilities:

1. Review and approve the fundamental operations, financial and committee charter.

2. Hold meetings regularly.

3. Develop an investment policy statement.

4. Evaluate the manager's performance and take appropriate actions.

5. Select and remove investment managers.

6. Monitor the activities of prudent experts.

7. Review investment management fees paid by the plan and participants.

8. Review procedures for providing financial and operational information to the board.

9. Document the investment process and decisions made.

In essence the investment committee is charged with developing the plan's long-term investment policy and carrying it out on a consistent basis. The resolve of the committee will be challenged in reaction to short-term market events; therefore, it is critical for investment committees to understand their role and maintain their discipline in fulfilling their fiduciary duties.

Defining a Prudent Investment Process for 401(k) Plans

As mentioned earlier, the duties of an investment committee are fiduciary in nature and, as a result, members of an investment committee are considered investment fiduciaries. As an investment fiduciary, you are required under ERISA to make investment decisions that are:

1. Prudent

2. In the sole interest of the plan participants and beneficiaries

3. Diversified to minimize the risk of large losses

4. In accordance with the plan document

Failure to satisfy these four standards can expose a fiduciary to personal liability (which includes home, personal assets, and business assets) for any resulting plan losses from breach of fiduciary responsibility. In fact, ERISA Section 409(a) states: "Any person who is a fiduciary with respect to a plan, who breaches any responsibilities, obligations, or duties imposed upon fiduciaries by this title shall be personally liable to make good to such plan any profits of such fiduciary which have been made through use of assets of the plan by the fiduciary, and shall be subject to such other equitable or remedial relief as the court may deem appropriate, including removal of such fiduciary."

ERISA does provide plan sponsors with relief under Section 404(c) for investment choices made by plan participants. However, it does not relieve a fiduciary/investment committee from liability for the selection and monitoring of the plan investment options. So how does an investment committee meet its ERISA duty? What procedures does it follow?

The first step to ensure compliance with ERISA standards is to establish and follow a well-defined investment process. Statutes, case law and regulatory opinion letters dealing with investment fiduciary responsibility further reinforce this important concept.

Compliance with your fiduciary responsibilities does not require that you have the best performing investment choices available to your participants all the time, with the lowest cost. The investment committee's primary role is to manage the process. That is, an investment committee's responsibility is to provide the essential management of the investment process, without which the other components of the investment plan cannot be defined, implemented, or evaluated (Center for Fiduciary Studies www.cfstudies.com).

Fortunately, there are resources available to fiduciaries for developing and documenting a formal investment process, by which they can prudently manage their defined contribution plan assets and substantially reduce their fiduciary liability. For example, the Foundation for Fiduciary Studies, which is an independent, non-profit organization, has published the *Prudent Investment Practices for Investment Stewards.*

Developed specifically for investment fiduciaries and those involved in investment–making decisions, the Foundation has identified three major legislative acts involving fiduciary relationships, including ERISA. The result was the following seven global fiduciary precepts (Ibid) for any fiduciary to follow:

1. Know standards, laws, and trust provisions.

2. Diversify assets to the specific risk/return profile of a client.

3. Prepare an investment policy statement.

4. Use prudent experts (money managers) and document due diligence.

5. Control and account for investment expenses.

6. Monitor the activities of prudent experts.

7. Avoid conflicts of interest and prohibited transactions.

If members of an investment committee are personally accountable by law for their actions, then adopting a consistent, disciplined and documented approach is critical to successfully managing their investment fiduciary responsibilities.

Chapter 2

FORMING AN INVESTMENT COMMITTEE

For any investment committee to succeed, there must first be a written charter outlining the roles and responsibilities of the committee members, support staff, and investment advisors or consultants.

Design of the committee structure will be dictated in large part by the terms of the company's respective plans and governing corporate documents (articles of incorporation, by-laws, and Board of Directors' actions and delegations of authority). It is important that the Board of Directors, or other governing body, clearly establish the authority of the committee (AON Fiduciary Fundamentals under the Employee Retirement Security Act [ERISA]).

Not only is it important for the board of directors to confer authority to the investment committee, but also it must take an active interest in the committee's actions. In recent years, the courts have clarified that corporate officers and board of directors (e.g., ENRON) who have the authority to appoint and remove committee members are acting as a fiduciary. As a result, they can be held accountable for the committee's action or lack of action.

The main purpose of the charter is to establish formally the rules, conduct, and expectations of the committee and its members. The goal is to keep the charter clear and concise so that the committee's goals and fundamental duties are easily understood and measurable. There are many forms of charters used today, and the best ones cover the following topics:

Purpose—The investment committee is established to be the investment fiduciary to the plan. It is solely responsible for developing and implementing an investment policy statement for the selection and retention of the investment options made available in the plan.

Roles and Responsibilities—These establish investment objectives and make investment recommendations in accordance with the plan's investment policy statement. This includes the monitoring of all investment and plan-related service providers, as well as the reasonableness of all expenses and costs in light of services being provided.

Status and Membership—These should address who's on the committee and which roles (chief financial officer [CFO], human resources [HR]) are permanent, who chairs the committee and how often the committee members are rotated out.

Meetings—These define how often the investment committee meetings will be held and action to be taken if members fail to attend regularly. The committee should meet quarterly to review reports from their investment advisor, plan provider, consultant, or third-party administrator.

Choosing the Right Investment Committee Members

Members of an investment committee are not born—they are selected. They are frequently chosen because of their position or experience in benefit administration, accounting, and legal or corporate finance. Given the varying level of skills and experience, it is best to start by recruiting individuals in your organization who have an interest or basic understanding of financial markets.

Success of a committee starts at the top. The investment committee should be comprised of senior members of HR, finance, and operations. Benefits experts suggest an odd number of voting members—usually three to seven individuals—because committees that are too large become unwieldy, and it becomes difficult to get anything accomplished. Ideally, the investment committee should be headed by someone with strong investment skills such as the CEO or the CFO. We also highly recommend that the financial advisor or consultant be included in a non-voting capacity.

The investment committee will be comprised of permanent and non-permanent members. For instance, the CFO and vice president of HR probably will be permanent members of the committee, whereas the other non-permanent members may rotate every three years. Members should be listed by title rather than by name to facilitate continuity. It is imperative that members rotating off the committee do so in staggered years to alleviate disrupting the operations of the committee. Avoid appointing employees as members as some form of reward, and avoid becoming too dependent on any individual committee member. Make sure members attend the meetings on a regular basis and take their roles seriously. It is also a good practice to have a subcommittee of employees representing various departments or business unites attend the meetings in a non-voting capacity to share their input on the plan and its investment offering. These employees can also be great advocates in support of the plan and the investment committee within their respective departments.

Requirements for Being an Investment Committee Member

Probably the number one requirement for members to fulfill effectively their fiduciary obligations is to make sure that they have reviewed the plan documents and understood the plan's investment strategy. Given the potential liabilities, both personally and to the company, it is critical that members acquire sufficient knowledge of plan documents and procedures to make an informed decision on behalf of the plan participants and their beneficiaries. Therefore, when drafting members for the committee, look to select individuals who will take this responsibility seriously. Remember, it is not essential that the individuals who serve on a plan committee be investment experts, but that they are willing to make the commitment to perform the duties of a fiduciary to the best of their abilities

When appointing an individual to serve as plan trustee or member of an investment committee, you should have that person acknowledge in writing that he or she accepts the position along with the duties expressed in the plan document and committee charter (see Appendix 3). That person should also be informed that he or she will not receive compensation for service and that the term will have no set time limit and will expire upon resignation or termination of employment.

Indoctrinating New Investment Committee Members

Whether you are creating an investment committee for the first time or selecting a new member to an established committee, an orientation program on fiduciary duties, plan document, plan procedures and service providers should be in place to educate the newest members.

New members need to know they have fundamental fiduciary duties of loyalty and impartiality; that they should act with prudence in deciding whether and how to delegate authority and in the selection and supervision of agents; that they should follow the plan document; and that they should incur only costs that are reasonable in amount and appropriate to the responsibilities of the plan.

The following is a set of basic responsibilities that all fiduciaries must follow under the Employee Retirement Income Security Act (ERISA):

Primary Tenets of Fiduciary Responsibility

Duty of Loyalty—ERISA requires fiduciaries of retirement plans to make decisions based solely on the best interests of plan participants. As long as the fiduciary can demonstrate with documentation that the employees' best interests were considered, a decision resulting in a loss to the participant doesn't necessarily mean that the fiduciary is in violation of ERISA.

Duty to Diversify—According to ERISA Section 404(a)(1) (c), a qualified plan must offer a diversified investment menu that allows participants to minimize the risk of long-term losses. Fiduciaries must display knowledge of the investment marketplace—meaning they are held to an expert standard. In areas where they may be deficient, fiduciaries are expected to consult with or even hire financial experts to help them conduct a thorough analysis of their plan investment offerings. These experts can then alert the fiduciaries to add certain asset classes or demonstrate that it is prudent not to have those asset classes.

Duty to Incur Only Reasonable Expenses—Committee members should understand that the expenses of their plan are reasonable when compared with the market. Determining whether expenses are reasonable does not mean that the expenses have to be the lowest; nor are fiduciaries automatically safe if their expenses are the lowest.

Duty to Provide Monitoring and Oversight— A committee can delegate or shift responsibility for managing the retirement plan's money to someone who's better qualified; they cannot delegate their duty to monitor the managers in a well-defined, consistent manner to ensure compliance with agreed on tasks, consistency of style, performance against benchmarks, and any significant changes. This oversight responsibility means it never goes away, and the penalties for abdicating that responsibility are pretty serious.

Duty to Avoid Prohibited Transactions—Prudent management and oversight of the plan includes safeguarding against activities that constitute a conflict of/or party in interest. Such activities might include the direct or indirect sale, exchange, or leasing of property; lending money or other extension of credit; and furnishing of goods or services. These include the direct or indirect sale, loan, exchange, or transfer of any plan assets. A fiduciary may not use plan assets for personal gain, may not engage in transactions on behalf of parties whose interests are adverse to the plan, and may not realize personal gain in connection with any plan transaction. For example, if a fiduciary has a close relationship with a person dealing with the plan, the true independence of that fiduciary may be open to challenge. Even the appearance of self-dealing should be avoided.

Pleading ignorance, bad communications, or inexperience will not be adequate legal defenses. Delegation to prudent experts and the proper overseeing of them are the only defenses on which a fiduciary can rely. The government's interest is in protecting the participant, not the fiduciary or plan sponsor. Virtually every time a conflict arises between the interests of the participant and those of the sponsor, legislation favors the participant.

Chapter 3

INVESTMENT COMMITTEE MEETINGS

Forming an investment committee signals that an organization has created a formal process to satisfy the Employee Retirement Income Security Act's (ERISA's) requirements for a prudent process. The committee should meet two or more times per year to review investment performance and carry out its functions. The person responsible for leading the committee is advised to gather all relevant investment material, reports from the plan advisor, and the issues to be addressed. This information, along with an agenda, should be distributed to the members in advance of the meeting. The meetings should be of sufficient length of time to allow all participants to review the issues, express their views, and reach a resolution.

Control of the Agenda

Typically, what will be discussed and acted on by the investment committee is determined initially by the committee's chairperson. Every committee member should have an opportunity to place items on the agenda, as well as to influence the priority and amount of time allocated to various matters. Further, committee members should be satisfied that there is an overall annual agenda or matters that require recurring and focused attention: for example, review of investment performance, required continuance of contract arrangements, required regulatory approvals, review of other services provided by the advisor and its affiliates, and meeting with the independent accountants of the plan.

Information Provided

The quality of information made available to committees significantly affects their ability to perform their roles effectively. During each meeting, sufficient information needs to be provided to allow the investment committee members to compare the actual performance results of the investments (funds or separate accounts) to the same data or benchmarks used in the investment policy statement (IPS). This review should include:

1. Recent and rolling performance of the investment option compared to its appropriate peer group and industry index

2. Risk adjusted performance (such as Alpha and/or Sharpe)

3. Changes, if any, to the portfolio management team

4. Dramatic increase or decrease in the investment offerings assets under management

5. Whether there have been any changes in investment style, indicating style drift

6. Whether the securities in the portfolio are consistent with the stated objective

7. Whether there has been a material change in management fees or associated costs

8. Regulatory concerns—whether the investment manager has been involved or cited for regulatory issues

To the extent feasible, this information should be concise and timely, well organized, and supported by any background or historical data necessary or useful to place the information in context. It should be designed to inform committees of material aspects of a plan's operations, its performance, and prospects, as well as the nature, quality, and cost of the various services provided to the plan by the investment advisor, its affiliates, and other third parties. Whenever possible, information should be provided in written form sufficiently in advance of the meeting to provide time for thorough review and meaningful participation by the committee.

Disagreements

Often investment committees will engage in consensus decision—making. Not wanting to rock the boat can create an environment where recommendations go unchallenged and further expose fiduciaries to potential liability. If there is disagreement with any significant action to be taken by the committee, the dissenting member may vote against the proposal and request that the dissent be recorded in the minutes. Under state law, a committee member is generally presumed to agree unless his or her dissent is so noted. Except in unusual circumstances, a dissenting vote should not cause a committee member to consider resigning. However, if a member believes that information being disclosed by the plan is inadequate, incomplete, or incorrect or that the advisor is not dealing with the committee members, the shareholders, or the public in good faith, that committee member should seek corrective action and consult with counsel for purposes of determining an appropriate course of action.

Documenting Deliberations

There should be a commitment to ongoing documentation so there is a clear process for recording the committee's activity and decisions. Keeping a written record of meetings assures continuity and accountability. Documentation is one of the most important actions a committee will take to demonstrate that a prudent process is being followed.

Keeping an accurate account of the decision made by an investment committee is fundamental to ongoing plan operations. That is why it is important that the investment committee report their activities clearly and accurately to the Board or to other persons in the company that the committee reports to by preparing minutes to meetings. The minutes do not have to be a word for word account of the proceedings (see Appendix 2). Instead, the minutes of the meeting should summarize issues discussed, recommendations made, actions taken, and committee members in attendance. Following are those items that should be included in plan minutes:

1. Date, time, and place where meeting was held—Include members who attended and those who did not. Include financial advisors, plan service providers, outside counsel, and other non-member guests.

2. Matters discussed—Include a copy of the agenda, presentations or recommendations given by advisors or plan providers, decisions made, and actions not taken or tabled for future meetings. Also, record each committee members vote.

At the beginning of each subsequent committee meeting, a copy of the minutes from the previous meeting should be reviewed and approved by the members in attendance. This will give members who were absent from the previous meeting an opportunity to go on record as agreeing or disagreeing with the actions taken. Committees should review and may also ask the plan's counsel to review draft minutes of the committee meetings before approving them.

Creating and Maintaining Plan Fiduciary Records

A central place for internal records should be maintained to build an audit file that is easily accessible for review and verification of compliance. External reports are required to satisfy plan participants, their beneficiaries, and regulatory authorities that assets are being properly administered and prudently invested. Specific steps concerning the functions necessary to the management of your plan should be followed and documented in writing.

As noted earlier, a fiduciary's primary responsibility should be focused on establishing a procedurally prudent investment process. This includes setting the investment policy, selecting the professionals to implement the process, and monitoring the results of the process. Therefore, a readily accessible fiduciary audit file will demonstrate that the process has been properly established and followed and will also document all significant decisions relevant to the plan.

Assume that in the future your committee's investment decisions will be examined in detail. Documentation is critical and spans a wide array of both internal and external reporting requirements. Such documentation includes journals, ledgers, account statements (including bank and trust statements), appraisals, and so forth that support all plan assets and investments.

Other items that should be maintained include (See Appendix 5):

- Analyses and reports from investment managers and consultants and performance measurement data

- Certificates, documents, statements of additional information (if a mutual fund), confirmations, and all necessary items depicting evidence of ownership in the plan assets/investments

- Annual copies of Form ADV for each money manager, along with certification by the manager that appropriate registrations are maintained under the Investment Advisors Act of 1940 and the State Securities Board

- Copies of Requests for Proposals (RFPs) and any competitive bid documentation along with all related correspondence and copies of service agreements and correspondence with current and former consultants, asset allocation advisors, recordkeeping and custodial providers.

The following best practices come from a Web cast (February 23, 2005) with Thornburg Investment Management and attorney Fred Reish. It was so right on the mark, that we obtained permission to include here Fred Reish's "Six Steps to Fiduciary Protection and Best Practices." The first four items are practical steps to minimize the risk of fiduciary liability. They are meant to be realistic rather than legalistic. In other words, they are real-world steps you can take to reduce risk. The last two steps are in the category of "best practices."

1. The plan committee should meet at least once a year.

2. There should be a written report covering, at the least, the plan investments. In a perfect world, it would also cover services such as participant investment advice, participant education, and so on. It should also cover data on the usage of those services and on the investment activities of the participants. The report could be prepared by either the plan provider or by the advisor.

3. The committee members should read the report and consider any applicable recommendations. The committee members need to understand the report well enough

to make informed decisions. They should ask questions where they do not understand and the advisor should either answer those questions or obtain the answers. Once the committee has reviewed the report and asked questions and received answers, it should make an informed and reasoned decision about the plan's investments and services. The committee members cannot rely blindly on the report. They must understand it and adopt it as their own. However, a report would ordinarily provide substantial evidence of due diligence.

4. Minutes of the committee meeting should be prepared and drafted in a conclusive style. They should be limited to citing the materials reviewed, the issues discussed, and the decisions made. The minutes, together with the report, should be placed in a due-diligence file.

5. As a best practice, the committee should discuss whether the plan is operating successfully. In other words, does the plan have a high level of participation, high rates of deferrals, and prudent participant investing?

6. As a best practice, the committee should review the investment policy statement and determine whether it continues to be appropriate for the needs of its plan and its participants. If it needs improvement, then it should be amended to reflect decisions regarding improvement of the IPS.

Chapter 4

IMPORTANCE OF INVESTMENT POLICY

The investment policy statement (IPS) is the cornerstone of the investment committee decision-making process and your safeguard. It describes the plan's investment strategy and ongoing review process. It also gives the committee structured processes for selecting money managers or funds and for identifying circumstances for removing an investment option. "The investment policy statement provides evidence that a clear process and a methodology exist for selecting and monitoring plan investments" (J. Gardner, *How to Write an Investment Policy Statement*).

Without a written description of procedures affecting the plan investments' decision-making, the plan sponsor has an obligation to provide evidence linking plan objectives and the proper exercise of fiduciary responsibility for every plan investment-related decision. The existence of an IPS provides evidence of a prudent investment decision-making process and plays a valuable risk management role as the first line of defense against potential fiduciary liability.

An IPS is a written document outlining the process for your committee's investment-related decision-making. It also provides a paper trail you may need if problems develop in the plan's future.

The IPS sets fund selection and retention standards, including the following:

- Processes—Decision system for analyzing and selecting plan investment managers

- Procedures—Integrated quarterly reporting for oversight of ongoing plan investment performance that is based on the standards set forth in the IPS

- Practices—Remediation methods for management of funds whose performances represent exceptions to the stated objectives of the plan

Further, a well-constructed IPS provides evidence that a clear process and methodology exist for selecting and monitoring plan investments. In fact, in the process of a plan audit, the Department of Labor will routinely ask to see a plan's investment policy statement within the initial audit notification and information request letter. The investment committee members who have not described the procedure required by the Employee Retirement Income Security Act (ERISA) in a written IPS and documented their implementation of investment-related decisions may render themselves vulnerable to legal action either from disgruntled plan participants or from the Department of Labor.

Section 402(b) of ERISA states: "all" employee benefit plans must include a procedure for establishing and carrying out a funding policy and method consistent with the objectives of the plan and ERISA. Though there is no ERISA requirement that a written investment policy be adopted by a plan, many ERISA experts believe that a plan should have an IPS. This is further supported by statements issued by The Department of Labor (DOL) that a written IPS is "… consistent with the fiduciary obligations set forth in ERISA" (DOL Interpretive Bulletin 94-2). The primary duty of the investment committee is to implement and execute the plan's investment objectives as delineated in the IPS.

Benefits of the IPS

In addition to the legal and regulatory reasons for adopting an IPS, the ever-increasing number and variety of defined contribution investment offerings are enticing to many plan sponsors.

An expansion of core investment offerings—including a variety of investment styles and disciplines, mutual fund windows, and self-directed brokerage products—all are available within today's defined contribution investment landscape. The IPS gives the investment committee a guide for navigating through these choices. Implementing an investment policy statement also has practical advantages for the investment committee. For example, an investment policy statement accomplishes the following:

- Helps clarify the plan's investment-related goals and objectives

- Provides a framework for evaluating investment performance

- Aids in clear communication of plan investment policy to participants

- Ensures continuity in decision—making as committee members and plan fiduciaries change

- Protects the sponsor from inadvertently making capricious or arbitrary decisions

- Helps the sponsor manage pressure for change generated by participants, vendors, or the media

Implementing the IPS

Who is responsible for creating and maintaining an IPS? Ultimately, this job falls squarely on the shoulders of the committee. Unbiased experts may be hired to provide services that accomplish many of these task elements, but the final responsibility rests with the investment committee.

When an investment committee adopts a written investment policy, follows its guidelines, and documents periodic plan investment reviews, the committee has created a roadmap identifying what is to be done, how it is to be done, and when it will be done. It provides a very important paper trail for the committee, should its decisions be challenged or investments not perform as well as expected.

An effective written investment policy will reduce the burden of following the policy by encouraging or, where possible, automating adherence and the monitoring process. Further, it will permit non-expert fiduciaries to integrate expert support easily for executing the duties that accompany the offering of a retirement plan.

The investment policy statement's content should always be customized to each committee and its specific needs. Some investment committees prefer to adopt a brief investment policy statement summarizing the critical aspects of their plan investment goals and decision-making processes, whereas others prefer a more detailed version, addressing topics more specifically.

Although no single approach is appropriate for every committee, following are a number of topical areas for consideration by investment committees that are embarking on developing a new or revising an existing:

Checklist

1. Types of investment options

2. Number of investment options

3. Fund selection criteria—defined process and methodology

4. Roles and responsibilities of parties involved in plan investment decisions

5. Criteria for selecting investment managers

6. Plan monitoring and evaluation criteria—defined process and methodology

7. Benchmarking against indexes and peers

8. Risk measurement

9. Fees

10. Plan reporting requirements

11. Extraordinary events

12. Options for plans that do not meet evaluation criteria

13. Decision to hold, add alternatives, or substitute funds

14. 404(c) compliance

15. Procedures for enforcing and amending the IPS

16. Investment communications and education for plan participants

For investment committee members to meet their legal obligation, they must prudently select and manage plan investment offerings. The implementation of a written investment policy statement ensures careful consideration of both the formulation and implementation of appropriate investment strategies. It will contribute significantly to the success of an employer's defined contribution program and go a long way to document the committee's current and future process.

Chapter 5

COMPLYING WITH ERISA SECTION 404(C)

Although investment committees have oversight responsibility for all aspects of the 401(k) plan—including writing an investment policy statement (IPS), selecting plan investment options, and monitoring expenses—to avail the protection of the Employee Retirement Insurance Security Act (ERISA) section 404(c), most committees will want each plan participant to be responsible for his or her investment selections among the options offered.

When participants exercise control over their accounts, they become fully responsible for their choices. Exercising self-direction does not mean the participant becomes a fiduciary of the plan with respect to such control. However, if the participant is unrestrained in his or her investment choices (i.e., if he or she can direct the trustee to open a brokerage account and buy any stock, real estate, bonds, etc.), and the plan meets certain administrative requirements, the participant becomes responsible for the results of his or her investment direction. That is, the participant cannot go back to the employer or investment committee when the investments perform poorly and claim a right to reimbursement because of a breach of fiduciary duty.

The general understanding among investment committees is that by offering a participant-directed plan, you do not have fiduciary responsibility: you have relinquished or mitigated the responsibility. However, not being in total compliance with ERISA section 404(c) might make your committee members liable for losses resulting from the investment selections and allocations chosen by the participants.

Transferring Investment Responsibility

Fred Reish, of Reish Luftman Reicher & Cohen, states that there are two reasons why companies often fail in their efforts to transfer fiduciary responsibility to the employees to the extent allowable. First, the responsibility for choosing and monitoring the investment options—as opposed to participants choosing among a pre-selected menu of investment options—cannot be transferred to the employees. Therefore, someone other than the employees chooses the investment options offered by the plan. This decision maker—the board of directors, a plan investment committee, an officer of the company—is the responsible fiduciary.

In selecting the investment options, the responsible fiduciary must act prudently and is liable for losses resulting from an imprudent decision. Second, to transfer responsibility effectively for selecting from among investment options, the plan must follow specific rules. These rules are in the Department of Labor (DOL) regulations under ERISA Section 404(c).

Ensuring ERISA Compliance

The regulations are not a safe harbor. To comply with ERISA Section 404(a) (1) (c), an investment committee must follow all of the terms and conditions of the regulations, including a few that are more form than substance. One consequence of this formalistic application of the regulations is that many employers who think that they adopted 404(c) plans may risk losing the protections of section 404(c) for relatively minor violations.

One violation stands out above all others: failing to tell participants that the plan is intended to be a Section 404(c). The regulations require that participants are told explicitly, including the fact that committee members may be relieved of losses that are the direct and necessary result of participant investment directions. Failure to comply with this requirement can result in unintended exposure or liability. Check with your advisor or plan vendor to see how this requirement is communicated to plan participants. Even if the vendor promises that the program is Section 404(c) compliant (and many do not), still, responsibility for employee communications frequently is left to the employer.

When issued in 1992, the regulations assumed a relatively simple model for Section 404(c) relief. A plan would offer a specific menu of at least three investment fund options (usually mutual funds or bank collective funds) chosen by fiduciaries. Participants would choose among those options every quarter. This model seems very old-fashioned from the vantage point of 2005 when plans routinely provided an average of 14 investment options, daily valuations, and investment switching with respect to a wide array of investment options. Increasingly, plans are moving away from the investment menu model to offer participants even greater investment control.

To meet the requirements of this ERISA Section[1], the investment committee must follow rules found in DOL Regulations 2550.404c-1.

The primary requirements of these regulations are that a participant or beneficiary must have the opportunity under the plan to do the following:

---

[1] DOL Reg 2550.404c-1. See also, Perdue, "ERISA Liability of Fiduciaries and Plan Service Providers Is a Growing Concern," 2JTEB 19 (May/Jun 1994), and Jenkins, "Fiduciaries of Participant-Directed Accounts Must Plan to Protect Themselves," 2JTEB 116 (Sept/Oct 1994).

- Receive a statement to participants of intent to be 404(c) compliant, including a statement that the investment committee may be relieved of certain liabilities.

- Review a list of investments (must be a minimum of three investment choices). Choose from a broad range of investment alternatives (the regulations require at least three or more diversified investment options that offer a variety of risk and return characteristics).

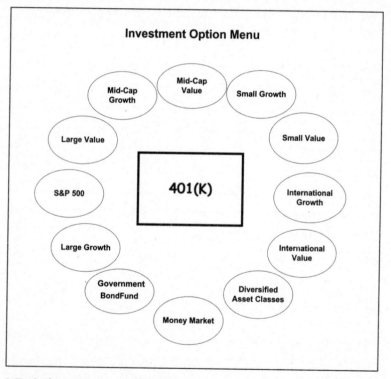

A Typical Investment Option Menu:

- Money Market
- Bond Fund
- Large Growth Fund
- Large Value Fund
- Small Company Fund
- International Fund
- Balanced Fund

- Be informed of the frequency of participants' ability to transfer assets among investment choices (quarterly is minimum).

- Review a description of investment alternatives, risk and return of each alternative, and a copy of the prospectus, when applicable. The current regulations do not require that a revised prospectus be delivered to each participant annually, so long as it is available on request (to the same extent it is available to the plan itself). However, many employers require plan sponsors to do so automatically to avoid subjective questions as to whether participants continue to make informed decisions.

- Be provided with instructions for how participants can request and obtain further information from the investment committee and investment managers.

- Have opportunity to review a record or log of plan participant information requests as well as how and when they were fulfilled.

Actions the Committee Should Take

Plan sponsors and committee members can limit their liability for participants by providing plan participants with sufficient education about the different investment options so each participant may make an informed decision appropriate to his or her circumstances.

Participant education should include information on investment managers including the following:

- A general description of the investment objectives and the risk and return characteristics for each investment option

- Information about the fees and expenses associated with each investment option

- A listing of securities held by each investment option

- Portfolio statistics (e.g., Alpha, Sharpe ratio and standard deviation) for each investment option

- Information on how to change investment strategy and allocation, ensuring that participants are clearly informed about how to make investment instructions and to whom

- A policy that relates to the use of company stock in the plan, if applicable

It is important to note, the participants must actually exercise control over such assets for ERISA Section 404(c) to be affected. Remaining in compliance with 404(c) is a process that must be managed continually. Only compliance with ERISA Section 404(c) can relieve the investment committee from liabilities arising from poor investment decisions made by the participant in a participant-directed plan. The test of 404(c) is whether your participants are now in a position to manage their own investments prudently.

If you are not sure whether you plan complies with 404(c), ask your service provider or financial advisor to help you satisfy the requirements. You may want to assign this responsibility to one other member of the investment committee to identify and correct any deficiencies.

Chapter 6

SELECTING, MONITORING AND REPLACING INVESTMENT MANAGERS

Of all the responsibilities an investment committee will undertake, none is as important as the selection of investment options offered to plan participants. In addition, although the Employee Retirement Insurance Security Act (ERISA) does not hold a plan fiduciary responsible for investment performance, it does require that a committee engage in a thoughtful decision-making process for choosing the investment options.

Committee Responsibility

Selecting the investment option of a plan requires that the investment committee follow ERISA's prudent man rule. As a practical matter, this requirement is met by constructing an investment menu that is diversified and provides all plan participants the opportunity to create a portfolio suited to their individual risk tolerance and investment schedule. This requires reviewing the appropriate information and considering all the facts and circumstances of each investment product and the needs of the participant before deciding which investment options are suitable for the plan and participants. In addition, a well-written investment policy statement (IPS) will provide a set of guidelines for the selection, monitoring, and—if necessary—removal of the investment manager or mutual fund.

It is recommended that the plan start by analyzing the current investments and the number of investment options in light of the following:

- Size of plan

- Employee demographics: age of group, education, income, and so forth

- Employees' understanding of investment concepts

- Plan's ability to monitor investment performance

- Suitability of investments for the particular needs of the plan

Working either alone or with help from a professional investment advisor, following a traditional investment management process will give the committee the framework for a sound due diligence process to fulfill their fiduciary obligation.

Selecting the Mutual Fund Manager(s)

The process of hiring mutual fund managers can be complicated and time consuming. Over the past decade, the landscape of investment choices inside a 401(k) plan has changed significantly. During this time, the number of investment options has more than doubled from an average of 6 to 14 funds for plan participants. Today, plan sponsors have more investment options to consider than in the past: core and non-core funds, lifecycle and lifestyle funds, brokerage accounts, and mutual fund windows. Therefore, the first step for the committee is to understand how these products work in relation to the needs of the plan participants.

As with other committee responsibilities, the use of a consultant or financial advisor can be very helpful in this process. Ultimately, your goal is to decide on the number of investment managers and which assets classes will be used, and define the performance criteria for making your selections.

Screening

An investment committee should have straightforward processes for hiring managers and for identifying the circumstances in which a relationship with a manager can be terminated. Generally, there are three key components for identifying potentially attractive investment options: (1) quantitative analysis, (2) qualitative analysis, and (3) fund review and monitoring.

A fund search should include quantitative as well as qualitative criteria. Morningstar, Ibbotoson Associates, Lipper and Standard and Poor's are companies that provide fund analytics to the investment professional community. Investment advisors and bundled plan providers use these and other software tools to rank fund performance versus funds in their peer groups. Whereas a committee's qualitative research will focus more on the mutual fund company's organization: the people, investment process and philosophy, manager tenure, fee disclosure, and so forth.

The fund selection process should begin with a systematic screening process to identify the universe of funds that meet the investment committee's specific criteria. Your chosen recordkeeper or service provider often defines this universe of investment choices. Though most plan providers tout an open architecture investment platform, in reality there is a finite number of mutual funds from which you can choose. Start by requesting a list of the funds available before beginning your search. Beginning with preferential asset classes and style group, the investment committee and its advisors determine the universe of funds that both possess the specific attributes required and generally reflect the quality of management and a solid investment process. This stage is purely quantitative, as the investment committee differentiates between what fits the investment policy statement (IPS) standards and what can be excluded easily.

An investment committee must determine which information it needs to review during the fund selection process. As noted earlier, there are a number of ranking and rating services that measure how a fund is doing in a number of key areas: past performance, expense ratio, and volatility. Given the emphasis on fund ratings, short-term market fluctuations, and the fear of being second-guessed, some committee members may be inclined to pick the highest ranked fund. Though fund ratings play a valuable role, they should not be the sole factor for selecting a fund.

Again, the IPS will help you manage the process by identifying the criteria for fund selection. Below is a list of factors to consider when conducting your due diligence of an investment manager. Your goal is to decide on the number of investment options, and to choose the asset classes per option and define performance criteria and objectives. Identify the appropriate index for each money manager and/or asset class. The one decision that is typically more difficult to make than which manager or asset class fund to hire, is when it is time to replace the manager or fund. When performance criteria are identified in advance, the decision is easier to manage and implement. The committee will apply the following due diligence criteria in selecting each money manager or mutual fund:

> **Regulatory oversight**—Each investment manager should be a regulated bank, an insurance company, a mutual fund organization, or a registered investment adviser.

Correlation to style or peer group—The product should be highly correlated to the asset class of the investment option. (This is a critical part of the analysis because most of the remaining due diligence involves comparison of the manager to the appropriate peer group.)

Performance relative to a peer group—The product's performance should be evaluated against the asset class index and the peer group's median manager return, for 1-, 3-, and 5-year cumulative periods.

Performance relative to assumed risk—The product's risk-adjusted performance (Alpha and/or Sharpe Ratio) should be evaluated against the asset class index and peer group's median manager's risk-adjusted performance.

Minimum track record—The product's inception date should be greater than three years.

Assets under management—The product should have at least $75 million under management.

Holdings consistent with style—The screened product should have no more than 20% of the portfolio invested in unrelated asset class securities. For example, a Large-Cap Growth product should not hold more than 20% in cash, fixed income, or international securities.

Expense ratios/fees—The product's fees should not be in the bottom quartile (most expensive) of their peer group.

Stability of the organization—There should be no perceived organizational problems; the same portfolio management team should have been in place for at least two years.

Regulatory issues—Investigate allegations of improper mutual fund practices or securities violations.

Fund Monitoring Procedures

The investment committee must be aware that ongoing review and analysis of investment managers is just as important as the due diligence implemented during the manager selection process. Although committees are not judged on an investment's performance, they generally do retain a responsibility to oversee the fund's investment performance and monitor investment practices.

The performance of investment managers will be reviewed on a quarterly basis. It is at the committee's discretion to take corrective action by replacing a manager if they deem it appropriate at any time.

The investment policy should include regular oversight and a process for ensuring appropriate action if funds fall out of compliance. Selected investment options are compared against appropriate benchmarks established in the IPS, such as performance of other comparable investment vehicles or relevant market indices. Quarterly reporting also allows investment committees to incorporate new investment information regularly, including fund news and opinions about changes in the marketplace. This strategy allows investment committees to spot quickly any anomalies or deficiencies in fund performance.

Review Process

In general, the best committees can do the following:

- Recognize that markets are cyclical and so there will be periods when a manager, or a group of managers, will do well and others when they will do poorly. An understanding of what drives those results helps committees to have constructive conversations with managers.

- Require, if necessary, that any outstanding issues be discussed in a written report. Such issues may arise during a manager's responses to questions during a committee meeting or in the normal course of business. The committee should monitor any issues and how—or if—they are resolved.

- Acknowledge potential pitfalls before they materialize. The performances of benchmarks and peer groups need to be scrutinized in addition to the performance of the manager's portfolio. Performance numbers can be time-period dependent and should be evaluated over multiple periods. In addition, a committee should recognize that there may be a difference between conventional measurements of performance and those the committee is using to assess the portfolio's progress. The portfolio's relative performance versus a benchmark or peer group may not be the most relevant analysis.

- Match the right time to the investment strategy. Applying a short time frame to analysis of a portfolio positioned for long-term results leads to poor committee decisions that, in turn, can harm the portfolio's ability to meet the established objective. Three years should be the minimum time for evaluating the performance of an equity manager, and longer periods should be used to evaluate the performances of more specialized strategies.

- Management turnover is often a clear-cut compliance issue—the very fact of a management change can cause a plan to fail the IPS standards. It is important to delve more deeply into what management turnover signals. In addition, it is for just such a case that an IPS allows for flexibility. Is the new manager the person who actually has been managing the fund the whole time? Does he or she have a successful record with another firm? If so, management turnover may be a non-event. Otherwise, it may be prudent to place the plan on a watch list and adopt a wait-and-see response.

- Value the importance of a fund manager's solid record of compliance with regulators.

Creating a Watch List Process

Establishing watch list criteria enables the plan sponsor to set a predetermined period before deciding whether to retain or replace a fund in the plan. Like the fund selection process, the reasons for removing a fund need to be specific and based on both quantitative and qualitative criteria.

If an investment option fails to meet the criteria set forth in the IPS, but in the opinion of the committee does not warrant replacement, a manager may be placed on a watch list, and a thorough review and analysis of the investment manager may be conducted under the following circumstances:

1. A manager performs below median for his or her peer group over a 1-, 3-, and /or 5-year cumulative period for at least 4 consecutive quarters

2. A manager's 3-year risk adjusted return (Alpha and/or Sharpe) falls below the peer group's median risk adjusted return

3. There is a change in the professionals managing the portfolio

4. There is a significant decrease in the product's assets

5. There is an indication the manager is deviating from his/her stated style or strategy

6. There is an increase in the product's fees and expenses

7. Any extraordinary event occurs that may interfere with the manager's ability to fulfill his or her role in the future

Remember, you should conduct both qualitative and quantitative fund manager reviews. Look beyond the numbers and evaluate fund managers using truly independent information. Finally, maintain a disciplined long-term approach while avoiding short-term thinking.

Chapter 7

EMPLOYER STOCK IN THE 401(K) PLAN

For publicly traded companies, the use of employer stock as an investment option remains a popular yet risky decision for plan sponsors. Some 71% of publicly traded firms provide company stock as an employee benefit, either through 401(k) or employee stock ownership plans, according to the Profit Sharing/401(k) Council of America. Like other plan investment choices, members of the investment committee have a responsibility to determine whether company stock is an appropriate investment for participants and monitor for any substantial and dramatic losses in value.

In recent years, participants in retirement plans have lost millions of dollars in retirement savings because of rapid depreciation in the value of their company stock holding. Enron, WorldCom, and Merck & Co are examples of firms that are being sued by employees for breach of fiduciary responsibility involving the oversight of company stock and concern about the prudence of investment. They question the conduct of the plan fiduciaries. Did they review whether the company stock continued to be a prudent investment option? Did the fiduciaries have information about the stock but fail to protect the participants? Did they fail to act in the best interest of the employees? Should the participants have had the ability to diversify out of company stock?

For the most part, having company stock in a retirement plan has its advantages: (1) it fosters employee ownership and alignment of interests with the employer, (2) it puts a portion of stock in "friendly" hands, (3) it is a favorable tax treatment for participants who take distribution in company stock, and (4) the company match in stock doesn't require cash. However, having a non-diversified investment, like company stock, can increase the volatility of an employee's portfolio, resulting in large losses and creating potential liabilities for plan sponsors if the stock falls in value.

Throughout this book, we have dealt with the issue of prudence and the need for full and proper disclosure. However, there are circumstances involving company stock that can create a conflict of interest that is problematic for an investment committee and for employees. Under the Employee Retirement Income Security Act (ERISA) "exclusive benefit rule," fiduciaries are required to act exclusively in the best interests of plan participants and beneficiaries. When acting in this role, plan fiduciaries cannot put their personal interests or the employer's interests ahead of the plan participants. On the other hand, corporate officers who serve on the investment committee may have competing duties: the fiduciary duty to disclose information to participants under ERISA and a duty not to disclose "insider information" under the U.S. Securities and Exchange Commission (SEC) rules. Individuals with access to material developments that can affect the firm's performance and stock prices are obligated to inform the plan fiduciary appointees and participants. Therefore, it is best to exclude the CEO and other corporate officers with access to insider information from the investment committee.

Of the plans that offer company stock as either an investment choice or a company match, participants have, on average, 41% of their 401(k) assets invested in their employers' stock (Hewitt Associates). These participants, maybe unknowingly, are exposing themselves to large risks. Directors, officers and committee members who act as ERISA fiduciaries are personally responsible for losses resulting from their imprudent conduct. The recent number of lawsuits involving company stock in 401(k) plans requires plan sponsors, committees, and corporate officers to be aware of the risks and implement a variety of best practices to protect against breach of fiduciary responsibility.

Best Practices for Plans with Employer Stock

- Exclude corporate officers and insiders from investment or plan committees.

- Use independent ERISA fiduciary to determine and monitor suitability of employer stock to avoid a conflict of interest for the board of directors and corporate officers with inside information.

- Review quarterly the stock's performance relative to selected peers and benchmarks.

- Remove restrictions on the sale or diversification of company stock in the plan.

- Review fiduciary insurance policies for adequacy of coverage and ensure compliance with Section 404(c) of ERISA.

- Educate plan participants on the risk of non-diversified investment; include explanation with the quarterly participant's statements.

- Use cash instead of company stock to fund the 401(k) match.

Scource: Jill Elswick, Employee Benefit News, December 2004

Rick Meigs, President, 401kHelpcenter.com, LLC.

Fred Reish, Taking Stock: The Most Dangerous Investment, February 2005; and Taking Stock: Managing the Risk of Company Stock, June 2003; Fiduciary & Investment Issues: Beyond the Basics, AON, March 2005.

Chapter 8

HIRING A PENSION CONSULTANT

I t is clear from the foregoing discussion that the investment committee is responsible for selecting and monitoring the plan's investment options. In doing so, the committee must satisfy the following four Employee Retirement Insurance Security Act (ERISA) standards: (1) act in the sole interest of the plan participants, (2) follow the "prudent man" rule, (3) diversify assets among a broad range of investment options, and (4) follow the plan document. The reality is that most plan sponsors, trustees and investment committee members are neither ERISA nor investment experts and so need the assistance of independent experts. Add to that the sweeping changes of the Pension Protection Act of 2006, lawsuits over excessive 401(k) plan fees, and market volatility, it is no surprise that plan sponsors are increasingly seeking expert advice and guidance from industry specialists. Working with the right advisor will help an investment committee understand, decide, and implement the appropriate course of action through a prudent process.

ERISA encourages the use of independent financial professionals, investment consultants and money managers to help trustees who lack the knowledge or experience in areas such as investment selection and manager retention. The courts have further emphasized that a fiduciary who lacks the requisite training and skills "…may retain a qualified independent expert provided he first determines the expert is independent, qualified and has undertaken a sufficient analysis to have an informed opinion," (Donovan v. Mazzola 716 F.2d 1226 [9th Cir. 1983]). Therefore, although the fiduciary has the exclusive authority to manage plan assets, that authority can be delegated to a professional if the plan so provides in writing.

However, it is important to distinguish between hiring an independent investment manager and an investment consultant/advisor. An *investment manager* is someone who is registered with the U.S. Securities and Exchange Commission (SEC) under the Investment Advisors Act of 1940 (unless exempt, as would be the case for most banks and insurance companies), and accepts, in writing, discretionary authority and liability for management of plan assets. By doing so, an investment committee will not be liable for the acts or commissions of such investment manager. However, an investment committee cannot simply eliminate its fiduciary exposure by retaining a money manager. The fiduciary committee and its members will need to demonstrate that a due diligence process is in place for prudently selecting and monitoring outside fiduciaries. This is when a qualified investment advisor can be a valuable resource to a plan.

The role of the investment advisor to a plan committee is to help identify the plan's needs both now and in the near future and provide guidance in selecting the vendors best suited for the plan and plan participants. In this role, the investment advisor or direct sold plan provider is not an investment manager who has discretion over how a portfolio is constructed, but he or she helps guide the plan in the selection of investments that are appropriate—with the investment objectives spelled out in the investment policy statement.

The role of the advisor to a plan has expanded in recent years from a product-based model to an advice-based approach. Because of the events of the past five years, the importance of working with advisors who specialize in ERISA plans has assumed far greater importance for plan sponsors. Today's advisors should be viewed not as sales people who happen to sell retirement plan services, but as specialists who can provide solutions to plan sponsors in a number of critical areas:

- Analyze the current plan and determine needs.

- Assist in vendor search.

- Benchmark current plan services to industry standards and other providers.

- Provide and review the investment policy statement.

- Perform due diligence reviews and analyses of investment performance.

- Conduct employee education meetings.

- Review and determine the effectiveness of employee education material.

- Review all plan fees and costs against industry standards and plans of assets size and number of participants.

- Provide fiduciary education.

The advisor is an important partner who helps the plan sponsor manage his or her ERISA fiduciary obligations. It can be difficult for key plan decision makers to select a qualified retirement plan professional. But, how do they know which advisor is right for their plan? Plan fiduciaries must remember that they have a duty to monitor the activities of the experts they hire. They should ask for references from other satisfied clients, for demonstration of specific service elements and deliverables, and for proven expertise and experience in support of qualified retirement plans similar to the plan in question.

The committee should also try to determine whether the consultant or advisor has a proven record. It is important to be familiar with the financial industry activities or affiliations with which a consultant's firm is involved. This will help determine whether the consultant may face potential conflicts of interest and whether he or she has the level of commitment to the desired services.

1. What professional credentials or designations do the consultants or advisors hold? One valuable benchmark is a professional designation salient to the delivery of a systemic risk management service. Many professional designations (CFP, CFA, ChFC and CEBS) exist that might bear upon these issues. One in particular is the Accredited Investment Fiduciary™ professional designation, introduced by the Center for Fiduciary Studies in October of 2002. This is the only designation that illustrates knowledge and competency in the area of fiduciary responsibility. Holders of the AIF® mark must complete a specialized program on investment fiduciary standards of care successfully and subsequently pass a comprehensive examination.

2. What resources (software, staff, and technology) do they use in servicing the plan?

3. Do they have references from plans of similar size, employee demographics, or industry?

4. Do they offer any performance guarantees?

5. What processes and procedures do they use to select and review investments?

6. What methods or tools do they use to monitor participation rates, contribution rates, and asset allocation goals?

7. How do they conduct enrollment and ongoing education meetings?

Additional Questions to Ask a Consultant or Investment Advisor

In addition, committees can follow the DOL[1] and the SEC recently released set of questions to assist plan fiduciaries in evaluating the objectivity of the recommendations provided, or to be provided, by a consultant/investment advisor. This is one more step that demonstrates the committee is following a prudent process, ensuring that fiduciary exposure is mitigated.

The answers to these questions should be recorded in writing and made a part of the due diligence process:

1. Are you registered with the SEC or with a state securities regulator as an investment adviser? If so, has the committee been provided with all the disclosures required under those laws (including Part II of Form ADV)?

---

[1]A report released (May 2005) by the staff of the U.S. Securities and Exchange Commission, raise serious questions concerning whether some pension consultants are fully disclosing potential conflicts of interest that may affect the objectivity of the advice they are providing to their pension plan clients. This lack of discloser could constitute potential conflicts of interest under the Advisers Act and these issues need to be monitored and disclosed to plan fiduciaries. Under the Investment Advisers Act of 1940 (Advisers Act), an investment adviser providing consulting services has a fiduciary duty to provide disinterested advice and disclose any material conflicts of interest to their clients.

The committee can check Part I of the firm's Form ADV by searching the SEC's Investment Adviser Public Disclosure site: *www.sec.gov/answers/formadv.htm*. The committee can search for an investment adviser firm on this site and view that firm's Form ADV. Investment advisers file Form ADV to register with the SEC and/or the states. Form ADV contains information about an investment adviser and its business operations. Form ADV also contains disclosure about certain disciplinary events involving the adviser and its key personnel: *www.adviserinfo.sec.gov/IAPD/Content/Iapd-Main/iapd_SiteMap.aspx*.

The investment adviser must furnish a copy of Part II of Form ADV. Currently, the IAPD database contains Forms ADV only for investment adviser firms that register electronically using the Investment Adviser Registration Depository. In the future, the database will expand to encompass all registered investment advisers—individuals as well as firms—in every state.

What if an investment adviser can't be located in IAPD? You might contact your state securities regulator. Go to *www.nasaa. org/QuickLinks/ContactYourRegulator.cfm* or send e-mail to the SEC's Public Reference Branch at *publicinfo@sec.gov*.

2. Does the investment advisor have relationships with money managers that he or she recommends, considers for recommendation, or otherwise mentions to our plan for consideration? If so, describe those relationships.

Typically, consultant/advisors will be one of the following three: (1) representing a consulting group or department affiliated with a brokerage firm, (2) representing an independent firm with a broker affiliate, (3) representing an insurance company subsidiary.

When consultant/investment advisors have alliances or financial or other relationships with money managers or with other service providers, the potential for material conflicts of interest increases, depending on the extent of the relationships. Knowing what relationships, if any, the consultant/advisor has with money managers may help the committee assess the objectivity of the advice the consultant provides.

3. Do you (investment advisor) or your related company receive any payments from money managers you recommend, consider for recommendation, or otherwise mention to our plan for committee consideration? If so, what is the extent of these payments in relation to their other income (revenue)?

Payments from money managers to pension consultants/investment advisors could create material conflicts of interests.

4. Do you have any policies or procedures to address conflicts of interest or to prevent these payments or relationships from being considered when providing advice to our plan committee?

5. If you allow our plan to pay their consulting fees using the plan's brokerage commissions, do you monitor the amount of commissions paid and alert plans when consulting fees have been paid in full? If not, how can you make sure we are not over-paying your consulting fees?

You may wish to avoid any payment arrangements that could cause the plan to pay more than it should in pension consultant fees.

6. If you allow plans to pay their consulting fees using the plan's brokerage commissions, what steps do you take to ensure that our plan receives best execution for its securities trades?

   Where and how brokerage orders are executed can affect the overall costs of the transaction, including the price the plan pays for the securities it purchases.

7. Do you have any arrangements with broker-dealers under which you or your related company will benefit if money managers place trades for our plan with such broker-dealers?

   You may wish to explore the consultant's relationships with other service providers to weigh the extent of any potential conflicts of interest.

8. If you are hired, will you acknowledge in writing that you have a fiduciary obligation as an investment adviser to our plan while providing the consulting services?

   All investment advisers (whether or not they are registered with the SEC) owe their advisory clients a fiduciary duty. Among other things, this means that advisers must disclose to their clients information about material conflicts of interest.

9. Do you consider yourself a fiduciary under ERISA with respect to your recommendations to our plan?

10. In what percentage do you use money managers, investment funds, brokerage services, or other service providers from whom you receive fees?

The answers to these questions may help committee members to evaluate the objectivity of the recommendations or the fiduciary status of the consultant under ERISA.

Generally, most plan sponsors believe their financial advisor to the plan is acting as a fiduciary. Unless you have authorized them to have discretion or control over plan assets, selection of investment options, or giving participants advice, you should think of them more as fiduciary consultants than as plan fiduciaries. One of the benefits to hiring an advisor is objectivity. Ideally, you want advisors who are independent—which means they do not represent just one service provider. They should be able to help you understand the variety of products in the marketplace and provide you with the latest advancements in products and services compatible with your plan needs.

Co-Fiduciary Services

A popular issue today with plans is the concept of a co-fiduciary. Under ERISA, co-fiduciaries are jointly and separately liable for one another's actions.

Today a plan sponsor can hire a person or firm that will *share* the fiduciary responsibility for (1) selecting mutual funds for their 401(k) plan, (2) performing ongoing due diligence of the selected mutual funds, including replacing those that do not meet the guidelines established in the investment policy statement (IPS), and (3) providing specific investment advice to plan participants. Anyone who gives investment advice is a fiduciary and thereby assumes co-fiduciary status with the plan fiduciaries.

Having a co-fiduciary can be extremely beneficial to a plan because it infers a sharing of liability, but there can be a sharing of liability only if the co-fiduciary accepts responsibility. As is the case with all fiduciaries, co-fiduciaries must be prudent and loyal to the extent that they exercise discretion or control over plan assets or plan management.

Most important, co-fiduciaries are liable for the fiduciary breaches of other plan fiduciaries if they (1) enable the breach, (2) participate in the breach, or (3) are aware of the breach and do not take reasonable steps to correct the breach. (ERISA Section 405(a)).

Many plan sponsors have confused (or have been led to believe) the meaning of co-fiduciary to mean that they have successfully delegated all plan fiduciary responsibilities to a third party. Not true. ERISA is clear that a plan cannot delegate or transfer all of its fiduciary obligations to a third party. Therefore, it is very important that you review carefully all documents and agreements that describe the nature of the services and acknowledge the vendors fiduciary status.

Sources:

Peter Swisher, "Solving an Employer's Fiduciary Dilemma: Liability, Discretion and the Role of the Qualified Plan Advisor

Chapter 9

FIDUCIARY LIABILITY INSURANCE

I t is important that plan fiduciaries have protection in the event of an alleged breach of the Employee Retirement Income Security Act (ERISA) fiduciary duty. Lawsuits brought by plan participants are increasing. It is important for a fiduciary who is *personally* liable for plan losses resulting from a breach of duty, as well as for breaches of other fiduciaries, to have a sound risk prevention program in place to minimize exposure. One method of protection is fiduciary liability insurance.

Fiduciary liability insurance protects fiduciaries against liability arising from violations of their fiduciary obligations, responsibilities, or duties under ERISA, including the selection and monitoring of investments. ERISA does not require the purchase of fiduciary liability insurance. However, due to the increased frequency and severity of ERISA lawsuits, many employers, both large and small, should secure this protection. ERISA *does* require a fidelity bond for individuals who handle plan assets. Too often, plan sponsors mistakenly assume that a fidelity bond provides fiduciary protection. It protects the plan from losses due to fraud or dishonesty, but not from other fiduciary breaches and liability claims.

Generally, fiduciary liability insurance is designed to protect the sponsoring organization, the retirement plan, and certain individuals (including the plan sponsor's directors, officers, and employees in their capacity as plan fiduciaries or administrators). Because fiduciaries can also be responsible for the actions of outside parties (experts) that provide plan administration, investments, or consulting services to the plan, coverage also extends to liability arising from certain acts, errors, and omissions in the administration of the plans. Fiduciary liability insurance policies typically cover the following costs: damages, judgments, settlements, defense costs, civil penalties of up to 5% imposed under ERISA Section 502(i) and up to 20% under Section 502(I), as well as certain settlements, fines, and penalties pursuant to various voluntary compliance and correction programs.

Related Coverage

There are a few things companies need to consider when purchasing liability insurance for plan fiduciaries. Fiduciary liability insurance pays, on behalf of the insured, legal liability arising from claims for alleged failure to act prudently within the meaning of the Pension Reform Act of 1974. Most directors and officers (D&O) insurance plans exclude coverage for ERISA claims. It is common to have both D&O coverage and fiduciary liability insurance. However, due to the increase of investor lawsuits and corporate governance legislation, premiums for D&O and fiduciary liability insurance have been increasing steadily. Insurers are addressing this issue by adding exclusions on fiduciary liability claims or imposing a shared dollar limit between the two policies.

A related insurance coverage is employee benefit liability (EBL) insurance. Like a fidelity bond, EBL does not protect against fiduciary liability. It covers errors that occur in the administration of a benefit plan. Because of other available insurance coverage like EBL, coordinating coverage among the various types of insurance is very important to managing fiduciary risk.

Managing Cost

Not all insurance carriers write fiduciary insurance and, for the most part, policy language is unique to each plan. There are several factors that influence the cost of fiduciary insurance coverage. Premiums vary depending on the type of plan, plan provisions and how the policy is structured. For an organization that sponsors a stand-alone 401(k) plan with good plan management and a diversified menu of investment options, the cost for insurance is competitive and reasonable. Under-funded defined benefit plans, converted cash balance plans, or plans with company stock will be higher.

Other key components of fiduciary insurance cost are defense control and deductibles. Like any insurance policy, the deductible is a function of the ability to pay versus the likelihood of occurrence. Plans that have confidence in their due diligence process will be willing to take on more risk and a higher deductible than those plans that do not manage the process well. For example, some employers have a fiduciary compliance audit completed by an independent party and use favorable audit results to negotiate lower premiums.

Many policies cover the defense costs and damages for breaches, but there are exclusions and limitations. For example, policies often do not cover claims arising out of profit-taking, fines and penalties, and deliberate or fraudulent acts. Defense coverage is a particularly important coverage feature. Plan trustees will have to decide whether to have the insurance company select counsel, known as "duty to defend," or use their own counsel. The latter, known as "pay on behalf of" gives the plan more control over the defense but may limit the insurer's willingness to pay. Each has advantages and disadvantages that the committee must consider.

Policy premiums can be paid with plan assets, by the employer, or by the individual fiduciary. Who pays for the policy will determine whether the insurer has recourse against the fiduciary. It is better if the company, rather than the retirement plan, purchases the insurance. If the plan purchases the fiduciary liability insurance with plan assets, then the insurer will have recourse against the fiduciary to recover any paid losses. This is good for the plan but not for the individual fiduciary. Fiduciaries can buy "nonrecourse" riders that prevent the insurer from seeking recourse and protecting the fiduciary against personal liability.

Rather than purchase liability insurance, the plan sponsor can indemnify the fiduciary. Under an indemnification agreement, the plan sponsor will agree to pay any losses or claims suffered by the fiduciary. Fiduciaries and plan sponsors should be certain they have a written indemnification agreement that addresses the broad range of issues that may arise if a claim is made against the fiduciary. Fiduciaries must bear in mind that the indemnification they receive is only as valuable as the plan sponsor's willingness and ability to pay any liability the fiduciary may incur.

The fiduciary liability market has seen dramatic increases in premiums and retentions, which are similar to deductibles, especially for plans with publicly traded stock. These changes are the result of the high frequency and severity of damages in ERISA lawsuits in recent years. Although these negative trends have leveled off somewhat for small to middle-market employers, the hardening fiduciary market for large employers is likely to remain in place for the foreseeable future. Nonetheless, fiduciary liability insurance can be an effective tool in protecting the plan and fiduciaries.

Sources:

Fiduciary Liability Loss Prevention, Chubb Specialty Insurance.

The Segal Company, Newsletter, November 2001.

Jill Elswick, Employee Benefit News, July 2003.

PlanSponsor.com, Tips on Securing Fiduciary Liability Insurance (Steve Saxon, Groom Law Group).

Mark Larsen, Tillinghast-Towers Perrin.

Chapter 10

UNDERSTANDING INVESTMENT EXPENSES & FEES

Fiduciary duties include ensuring that fees and expenses paid from plan assets are reasonable. But what is reasonable, and how does a plan determine plan costs? Experience shows that in most cases, plan sponsors do not understand or know fully the fees that the plan and its participants are paying on a direct or indirect basis.

Fortunately, the retirement plan industry and plan advisors are striving to fully disclose investment and recordkeeping costs to plan sponsors. Also, the U.S. Department of Labor (DOL) has issued guidelines and fee disclosure forms encouraging plan sponsors to take a greater interest in controlling and accounting for fees. Plan fiduciaries that do not follow the guidelines, or worse yet, do not know what they are, may be at risk.

Members of an investment committee have a fiduciary duty to inquire about, identify, and understand the costs associated with their plan. Are the purchased services necessary for the plan? Is the plan getting the desired or promised results? Is paying expenses consistent with the "exclusive benefit" rule and other fiduciary obligations of the Employee Retirement Income Security Act (ERISA)? Are the expenses incurred and paid from plan assets related to plan administration, or associated with settler expenses (E.g., decisions related to plan design, plan amendments or termination, and so forth), which may not be paid from plan assets?

Fiduciaries who do not take their fiduciary responsibilities seriously and are unable to demonstrate that plan costs are reasonable could cause losses to the plan and put themselves personally at risk.

As a result, plan fiduciaries must determine whether the plan is receiving sufficient services to justify payments that the service provider is receiving from the plan in the following manner:

- Identify all current plan expenses—including hidden expenses.

- Benchmark those expenses against those for similar plans.

Caution: there are many moving parts, and getting providers to disclose their pricing structure can be challenging.

Getting Started

Making sense of the myriad fees associated with a retirement plan is a difficult task for any investment committee. However, the long-term benefits to the plan and participants in terms of lower cost and larger account balances can be significant.

Basically 401(k) plan fees are divided into two broad categories: plan administration and investment management.

> **Plan Administration Expenses**—Obviously, there are costs associated with administering the plan. Administrative fees are usually calculated on a per-participant basis. In addition, the plan may offer extra services to employees such as education or investment advice. The plan may pay for

these expenses directly from the plan or from the general assets of the plan sponsor. Usually these expenses account for less than 10% of the total expenses of the plan.

Investment Expenses—The bulk of the plan's expenses can be attributed to investment expenses. These fees are more difficult to understand because often, they are deducted as a percentage of assets from the plan or directly from the fund—and at times—include additional fees that the plan participant will never see because the investment advisor collects these fees directly. Fees in this area vary widely and can be as much as two or three times more expensive, depending on the particular platform or product.

To determine where fees come from, a plan sponsor should first work with a comprehensive fee disclosure worksheet and be aware of the following types of fees:

1. *Hard Dollar Fees:* These expenses generally are easy to determine. Simply look at the plan and determine how much vendors are charging either on a per-participant basis or in the aggregate. Typically, these are the expenses charged by the bundled service provider on third-party administrator to document the plan and by investment advisors.

2. *12b-1 Fees:* This is a hot area these days. 12b-1 fees are charged based on the Securities and Exchange Commission (SEC) rule allowing investors to receive savings through certain economies of scale. Many registered investment advisors capture some or all of these 12b-1 fees as compensation in exchange for investment or education services they provide to the plan.

3. *Revenue Sharing Fees:* These fees might include sub-transfer agent fees, commission or finder fees, share class fees, and many other fees paid to the fund or out of the fund to service providers or to the money management companies. Revenue-sharing fees are a significant source of a fund's expenses and often the most difficult to determine.

Indirect Expenses

In addition to direct expenses, plans pay indirect expenses that reduce the investment returns. Evaluate the appropriateness of indirect expenses. Indirect expenses are a payment from plan assets just as if the plan's fiduciaries had written a check from the plan (DOL Technical Release 86-1).

Indirect expenses usually take at least one of the following seven forms:

1. *Mutual Fund Expense Ratios:* The returns reported by mutual funds are reduced by the costs of running the fund. The expense of operating a fund is established and reported as a percentage of the value of the assets in the fund. For instance, an expense ratio of 125 basis points is 1.25% of the value of the assets in the fund. Therefore, if a fund had gross earnings of 9%, it would report a return of 7.75%. Expense ratios are comprised of the cost of operating the fund as well as other costs such as 12b-1 fees and sub-transfer agent fees. It is essential that plan fiduciaries understand the level of these fees and determine whether the fees are reasonable compensation for the services delivered to the plan and its participants.

The costs of operating a fund include all expenses of the management and administration of the fund. Therefore, one would generally expect that the expenses of operating an indexed fund (which is passively managed) to be lower than the expenses of operating an actively managed fund.

2. **12b-1 Fees:** What are your mutual fund 12b-1 fees? Often the 12b-1 fees are often used to offset the plan's record-keeping and administrative costs. For a new plan with few assets, such an arrangement is, ordinarily, beneficial for the participants. However, as the assets grow, the fiduciary should periodically determine whether it is more advantageous to pay for the recordkeeping and administrative costs on an a la carte basis, switching to mutual funds or share classes that have lower expense ratios, and reducing the overall expenses of the investment program.

12b-1 fees are part of the expense ratios reported by mutual fund managers. 12b-1 fees are assessed to provide money for mutual funds to pay distribution fees (i.e., commissions) to brokers who sell the mutual fund shares and to pay for services provided to mutual funds. A fund is required to disclose its maximum 12b-1 fee in its prospectus.

Beginning in 1980, the SEC authorized mutual funds to charge 12b-1 fees to provide incentives for brokers to sell and service mutual funds to (1) increase the assets under management by mutual funds, (2) spread fixed costs over more assets, and (3) reduce expense ratios for the benefit of existing shareholders. Although the original rationale for 12b-1 fees was based on lowering overall investment management fees and expenses, experience has proven to be starkly different. According to a Morningstar analysis, expense ratios for the majority of funds that charge 12b-1 fees have actually increased over the past 10 years, raising questions about whether these fees really benefit shareholders (Traulsen, Christopher J. "Are 12n-1 Fees Being Abused," Morningstar Mutual Funds, Vol. 46, Iss. 3, p.1., January 6, 2004).

The new Rule 12b-1 amendments also require mutual funds to have policies and procedures in place on the use of directed brokerage for other purposes to prevent the mutual fund's investment manager from using directed brokerage to compensate a broker for promoting or selling mutual fund shares.

3. **Finder's Fees:** A finder's fee is a front-end commission paid on an initial investment and on subsequent deposits to the plan investment advisor. It is paid by the mutual fund company and is not incorporated in the fixed expense ratio the way a 12b-1 is.

4. **Revenue Sharing:** Revenue sharing describes money transferred from an investment manager (or mutual fund company) to a third party providing 401(k) recordkeeping and administrative services. Like expense ratios, these expenses usually are expressed as a percentage of plan assets. For example, a fund or manager may pay 25 basis points (0.25%) to the plan's recordkeeper. Revenue sharing reduces a fund's reported returns, is considered a payment from plan assets, and must follow ERISA's rules on the use of plan assets.

A typical 401(k) plan's assets will grow more quickly than the cost to provide core recordkeeping and administration services. Historically, the recordkeeper has kept this excess revenue generated by the growth of the plan. By knowing the cost structure of the plan and knowing exactly how much the provider is receiving in fees from the investments selected, the plan sponsor can negotiate a pricing contract that will return the excess revenue back to the plan. Typically, this excess revenue is returned either directly in the form of reduced investment expenses (e.g., lower-cost institutional share pricing) or indirectly in the form of a service credit that can be used to pay for qualified plan expenses such as legal and consulting fees, employee education or investment advisory fees.

The DOL has issued two opinion letters describing the conditions under which a Section 401(k) plan recordkeeper can accept revenue-sharing payments from mutual funds offered to plan participants without violating ERISA's conflict of interest rules (Other asset-based fees include shareholder servicing fees and sub-transfer agency fees).

The first advisory opinion says that recordkeepers have no ERISA conflict of interest problem if the recordkeeper's compensation remains the same regardless of which mutual funds are selected (DOL Advisory Opinion 97-15A).

In this case, the recordkeeper used the mutual fund payments to pay recordkeeping fees it would have otherwise charged to the plans, and the plans were entitled to mutual fund payments in excess of their recordkeeping fees.

The second advisory opinion indicates that recordkeepers have no ERISA conflict of interest problem if they are not acting as fiduciaries with regard to the selection or retention of the mutual funds as plan investment options (DOL Advisory Opinion 97-16A).

A recordkeeper could accept the payments from the mutual fund, even though its recordkeeper's compensation would depend on the funds in which the plan assets are invested. In both opinion letters, the DOL reminded plan sponsors of their fiduciary duty to decide whether the total compensation paid to the recordkeepers is reasonable and to obtain sufficient information about the recordkeeping fees and mutual fund payments to make informed decisions. (The DOL later issued similar rulings: DOL Advisory Opinion 2003-09A and DOL Information Letter (January 6, 2004)).

There is a new but growing trend in the defined contribution 401(k) marketplace known as "Revenue Sharing Pricing;" and for middle-market plan sponsors looking for a way to control and reduce the long-term costs of their defined contribution retirement plans, it represents a significant positive development.

What if you were the sponsor of a $35mm 401(k) plan and knew that the cost to provide all of the standard services was about 30 basis points including profit? If you know the cost of the plan, then you need to know what happens to the revenue generated in excess of 30 basis points. Knowing the cost of the plan allows smart plan sponsors to create a pricing model that will drive down the long-term pricing of the plan.

5. *Sub-Transfer Agent Fees:* A transfer agent is employed by a mutual fund to maintain records of shareholder accounts and disburse dividends, and send shareholder account statements, federal income tax information, and other shareholder notices. Transfer agents, usually banks or trust companies, can delegate certain recordkeeping and administrative tasks

to a sub-transfer agent for a fee. For example, a 401(k) plan recordkeeper could receive sub-transfer agency fees for handling recordkeeping and administrative tasks that would otherwise be performed by the transfer agent. Sub-transfer agency fees usually range from 5 to 25 basis points and are built into the mutual fund's expense ratio.

6. *Wrap Fees:* In some cases, plan service providers assess a so-called "wrap" fee. Typically found in group anuity contracts of plans administered by insurance companies, these fees are not referred to as wrap fees in formal documents. Wrap fees are an additional charge to plan assets and must be understood and evaluated by plan fiduciaries. For instance, a service provider may charge a 1.25% fee in addition to expense ratios. The plan fiduciaries must determine whether this additional fee is appropriate and necessary for the plan.

7. *Soft Dollars and Directed Brokerage:* The soft-dollar fees are very difficult to discern and determine because typically, they are deducted from the investment return of the fund and not listed expressly as a direct expense of the fund for the participant. These expenses often are disclosed in the prospectus, but some of the revenue-sharing fees are extremely difficult to find and the analysis should be undertaken by an expert professional. Once the total fees are understood, a plan can consider the lost opportunity cost due to its expenses.

Increasingly, plan sponsors are demanding—and service providers are disclosing—the fees charged to the plan. Your objective should be to determine if the services being rendered are reasonable relative to the cost to the plan as opposed to paying the lowest price. Plan related fees should be reviewed annually with a more in-depth review every three to five years. This will enable the committee to take into account increases in plan assets, number of participants, as well as new product and service features and technology enhancements that can have a significant impact on cost or benefits of plan participants. Becoming familiar with the direct and indirect components of plan expenses that affect the cost to the plan will serve you well in your role as investment steward of the plan.

Appendices

Appendix 1

INVESTMENT OPTION EVALUATION FORM

Name of investment option: _____

For mutual funds, also include ticker: _____

Broad Asset Class: _____ Peer Group: _____

Source of data: _____ Data as of: _____

Suggested Fields of Due Diligence	Yes	No
Regulatory oversight: Is the investment option managed by: (a) a bank; (b) an insurance company; (c) a registered investment company (mutual fund); or, (d) a registered investment advisor?		
Correlation to style or peer group: Is the investment option highly correlated to the asset class being implemented?		
Performance relative to a peer group: Is the investment option's 1-year performance above the peer group's median?		
Performance relative to a peer group: Is the investment option's 3-year performance above the peer group's median.		
Performance relative to a peer group: Is the investment option's 5-year performance above the peer group's median.		
Performance relative to assumed risk: Is the investment option's risk-adjusted performance (Alpha and/or Sharpe Ratio) above the peer group's median risk-adjusted performance?		

Minimum record: Does the investment option have at least a three-year performance record?		
Assets in the product: Does the investment option have sufficient assets under management (at least $75 million)? (Can include assets in related share classes.)		
Holdings consistent with style: Are at least 80% of the underlying securities consistent with the broad asset class? (For example, a Large-Cap Growth product should not hold more than 20% in cash, fixed income and/or international securities.)		
Expense ratios/fees: Are the investment option's fees fair and reasonable? (Suggested threshold: Fees should not be in the bottom quartile [most expensive] of the peer group.)		
Stability of the organization: Has the same portfolio management team been in place for at least two years?		
Stability of the organization: Are there any organizational issues that could affect the performance of the investment option?		

Appendix 2

SAMPLE INVESTMENT COMMITTEE MEETING MINUTES

Date: _____Time: _____

❏ Regularly scheduled   ❏ Special

Attendees (list):

Was there a quorum? ❏ Yes ❏ No

Matters discussed:

Materials reviewed:

Decisions voted:

Appendix 3

SAMPLE FIDUCIARY ACKNOWLEDGMENT LETTER

(Date)

(Address of Fiduciary)

SUBJECT: Appointment to Investment Committee

Dear (Fiduciary):

You are hereby appointed to serve as a member of the Investment Committee. As such, you will be serving as a fiduciary with specific duties and responsibilities. I have included a guidebook titled, *Best Practices for Investment Committees*, which outlines these duties and responsibilities. You are to become familiar with the contents and inform me of any questions and/or concerns you may have regarding your function.

You may be wondering what it takes to be a successful member of the Investment Committee:

> It does not require extensive experience in securities analysis or portfolio management, but it does require a personal interest in understanding the basics of capital markets and investment management procedures.

It requires a sincere commitment and the courage to develop a consensus formulation of goals and objectives with your fellow committee members; the discipline to develop long-term investment policies; the patience to evaluate events calmly in the context of long-term trends; and an understanding of personal and organizational strengths and weaknesses to determine whether delegation and outsourcing is more appropriate.

Most important, it requires the ability to get the right things done, otherwise known as effective management. A prudent investment process facilitates effective management by distinguishing important from unimportant tasks.

Please acknowledge receipt of this letter and your understanding of your fiduciary duties and responsibilities by signing and returning a copy of this letter to me.

Sincerely,

(Plan Sponsor, Trustee)

☐ I hereby accept my appointment to serve as a member of the Investment Committee. I understand the fiduciary duties and responsibilities associated with my appointment.

_____
Signature   Date

Appendix 4

BY-LAWS AND OPERATING PROCEDURES FOR THE INVESTMENT COMMITTEE

Section 1: FORMATION OF THE INVESTMENT COMMITTEE

1.1. Functions of the Committee

The Investment Committee (Committee) shall be the investment fiduciary responsible for the prudent management of the Investment Portfolio (Portfolio). The Committee will comply with all applicable fiduciary, prudence, and due diligence requirements experienced investment professionals would utilize, and with all applicable laws, rules and regulations from various local, state, federal and international political entities that may affect the Portfolio. The Committee shall have the exclusive authority to establish, execute, and interpret an investment policy statement for the Portfolio. The Committee shall be solely responsible for the selection and retention of professional advisors to the Portfolio, which may include, but not be limited to, investment managers, investment consultants, custodians, attorneys, accountants, and clerical staff.

1.2. Definition of a Fiduciary

A fiduciary is defined as a person who has the legal and/or implied moral responsibility to manage the assets of another person. A fiduciary must act solely in the best interests of that person. The Committee is subject to certain duties and responsibilities, including, but not limited to the following:

1. Knowing the standards, laws and trust provisions that affect the investment process of the Portfolio

2. Prudently diversifying the Portfolio to a specific risk or return profile (Or in the case of a participant-directed retirement plan, to make sufficient asset classes available so that a participant can prudently diversify his or her portfolio)

3. Preparing, executing, and maintaining an investment policy statement

4. Having investment decisions made by prudent experts

5. Controlling and accounting for all investment-related expenses

6. Monitoring the activities of all investment-related service vendors

7. Avoiding conflicts of interest and prohibited transactions

1.3. Establishment of Committee

The Committee shall consist of such number of individuals as are appointed by the Sponsor. Any member of the Committee may resign, and his or her successor, if any, shall be appointed by the Chairman. Each Committee member will acknowledge the acceptance of appointment to the Committee in writing. No Committee member shall have the authority to bind the Committee in any contract or endeavor without the expressed written authority of the majority of the Committee members.

1.4. Establishment of Offices

The Committee shall have an office of Chairman and a Secretary. The Chairman shall be responsible for the conduct of all the meetings of the Committee and shall have voting rights the same as any other Committee member. The Chairman shall perform such other duties as the Committee may assign and shall be the designated Agent for service of legal process.

The Secretary shall be responsible for keeping minutes of the transactions of the Committee and shall be the official custodian of records of the Committee. The Secretary, together with the Chairman, shall execute all official contracts of the Committee. The Secretary shall compile Committee agendas. The Chairman and the Secretary are authorized by the Committee to execute any instruments necessary for the Committee to conduct business.

1.5. Disclosure and Conflict of Interest

Notwithstanding any provision of law, no Committee member shall vote or participate in a determination of any matter in which the Committee member shall receive a special private gain. Committee members have a duty of loyalty that precludes them from being influenced by motives other than by the accomplishment of the purposes of the Portfolio, Committee members, in the performance of their duties, must conform and act pursuant to the documents and instruments establishing and governing the Portfolio.

Section II: MEETINGS
2.1. Attendance at Board Meetings

The Committee shall set its own schedule of meetings. Special meetings may be called by the Chairman or by a majority of the Committee members. The Committee shall meet at least once each quarter. Notices of meetings shall not be required if waived by all members of the Committee. In recognition of the importance of the work of the Committee, regular attendance at the Committee meetings is expected from all members. Any member who fails to attend two consecutive meetings of the Committee without an excuse acceptable to the other Committee members shall be deemed to have resigned from the Committee. A majority of the members of the Committee at the time in office shall constitute a quorum for the transaction of business. The action of the Committee shall be determined by the vote or other affirmative expression by the majority of its members in attendance where a quorum is present.

2.2. Agendas and Other Meeting Materials

An agenda shall be prepared for each regular and special meeting of the Committee. The agenda shall set forth those items upon which the Committee anticipates taking action or discussing. Each agenda item shall have attached backup material necessary for discussion or action by the Committee. A copy of the agenda and backup material shall be furnished to each Committee member prior to commencement of the meeting. Full and complete minutes detailing records of deliberations and decisions shall be maintained and held by the Secretary. The Secretary shall record all acts and determinations of the Committee and all such records shall be preserved in the custody of the Secretary. Such record and documents shall be open at all times for inspection by Committee members or for the purpose of making copies by any person designated by the Sponsor.

2.3 Rules of Order

In recognition of the importance of accomplishing the objectives of the Committee in a most orderly fashion, the Committee may establish rules of order or bylaws for the conduct of its meetings.

2.4 Appearance before the Committee

All persons who are scheduled to make appearances before the Committee shall be scheduled through the Secretary, and the Committee may establish the time limits established for such meetings. Appearances before the Committee may be in person or through a representative. All communications with the Committee shall either be in writing to the Secretary, teleconference, or by personal appearance at a Committee meeting.

Appendix 5

FIDUCIARY AUDIT CHECKLIST

At a minimum, the following documents should be collected and kept in your fiduciary audit file, which should include a section for each of the following categories of documents:

1. Plan Documents
Keep all plan trust documents, including a summary of any material modifications along with all amendments, addenda, and adoption agreement (if you have a prototype plan) and your summary plan description.

2. Government/Regulatory Requirements and Communications
Keep a copy of Internal Revenue Service Form 5500 and your audited financial statements that accompany the 5500s and any applicable notes. Include a copy of summary annual reports and trustee reports from the past six plan years.

3. Journals and Ledgers
Maintain journals, ledgers, account statements (including bank and trust statements), appraisals and other evidence to support all assets and investments.

4. Section 404(c) Compliance
Diversify your plan to comply with ERISA Section 404(a) (1)(c). Include a list of investments offered to plan participants (must

include a minimum of three diversified core investment choices); a description of the frequency of the participant's ability to transfer assets among investment choices (quarterly is minimum); a copy of the statement to participants of intent to be 404(c) compliant; a description of investment alternatives, risk, and return of each alternative and a copy of the applicable prospectus; and your record or log of plan participant and information request forms and how they are fulfilled. You should also include the instructions to participants on how to obtain further information.

5. ERISA Fidelity Bond

Place a copy and a quick reference to the amount of your plan's Fidelity Bond Policy. The amount of the bond must be at least 10% of the value of the plan assets, but not less than $1,000. The ERISA bond is not required to, but may exceed $500,000.

6. Participant Communication Documents Regarding 401(k) Education/Enrollment

Keep enrollment forms and procedures, loan and hardship withdrawal forms and claim procedures, rollover requests forms, plan distribution forms, and samples of participant account statements and other administrative forms you might use. Keep your entire 401(k) plan promotional materials, including copies of all plan marketing materials that document all investment options and related changes since the inception of the plan. Also, retain any participant communications from the plan administrator or plan sponsor and file your mutual fund prospectus here. In other words, any material relating to the investment options provided to your participants goes under this section.

7. Investment Policy Statement

The investment policy statement (IPS) is used as the business plan and the communication device for directing the activities of the investment program. Keep a copy of the IPS detailing the following information: (1) evaluation of the specific needs of the plan and its participants; (2) investment objectives and goals of the plan; (3) definition of the duties and responsibilities of all parties involved; (4) due diligence criteria for selecting investment options for the plan; (5) classes, styles and restrictions on investments authorized; (6) standards and benchmarks of investment performance for comparison; (7) policy and procedures related to the hiring, monitoring, and replacement of investment managers; and (8) procedures for monitoring and controlling investment expenses.

8. Third Party Service Providers

Save copies of all investment management agreements and related correspondence to current, former, and potential managers. Keep whatever documentation of the due diligence process was used to select investment managers. Maintain investment manager reports on performance, fees, and compliance to investment guidelines along with periodic reviews and monitoring of investment manager performance.

If you engage a consultant, document his or her recommendation in the areas of asset allocation, recordkeeping and custodial service. Keep copies of your requests for proposals (RFPs) and any competitive bid documentation along with all related correspondence and copies of service agreements and correspondence with current and former consultants, asset allocation advisors, recordkeeping and custodial providers.

9. Minutes of Meetings

Track investment and administrative committee meeting minutes.

This checklist was developed as a general guide. Therefore, each plan may have unique internal and external reports that must be retained. Consult your attorney or advisor for specific advice.

Appendix 6

GLOSSARY

The following chart breaks down the type of fiduciary accounts or entities to help organize and understand how legislation and oversight is overlaid.

Type of plan	Corporate Retirement (Defined Contribution and Benefit)	Public Retirement (Defined Contribution and Benefit)	Taft-Hartley (Defined Contribution and Benefit)	Foundation/ Endowment/ Eleemosynary	Individual/ Private Trust
Legislation	ERISA	MPERS	ERISA	UPIA	UPIA
Oversight	DOL, IRS, PBGC	State Attorney General	DOL, IRS	State Attorney General	State Attorney General

AIMR Performance Presentation Standards (AIMR-PPS): These are recognized as the leading industry standards for ethical presentation of investment performance results. The AIMR-PPS standards promote fair representation and full disclosure in every firm's presentation of its performance results to clients and prospective clients. The Standards were designed to ensure uniformity in performance reporting so that results are directly comparable among investment managers.

Asset allocation: The decision as to how a customer should be invested among major asset classes in order to increase expected risk-adjusted return. Asset allocation may be two-way (stocks and bonds), three-way (stocks, bonds and cash), or many-way (i.e., value mutual funds, growth mutual funds, small mutual funds, cash, foreign mutual funds, foreign bonds, real estate, and venture capital).

Balanced Index: A market index that serves as a basis of comparison for balanced portfolios. The balanced index used in the Monitor is comprised of a 60 percent weighting of the S&P 500 Index and a 40 percent weighting of the SLH Benchmark: A standard by which investment performance or trading execution can be judged. The most widely used performance benchmark is the total return of the S&P 500.

Bond Index (Government/Corporate): The balanced index relates unmanaged market returns to a balanced portfolio more precisely than either a stock or a bond index would alone.

Cash Sweep Accounts: A money market fund into which all new contributions, stock dividend income, and bond interest income is placed ("swept") for a certain period. At regular intervals, or when rebalancing is necessary, this cash is invested in assets in line with the asset allocation stipulated in the IPS.

Cash Profit Sharing Plan: A type of profit sharing plan in which the company contributes directly to employees in cash or stock. (This type of profit sharing plan is not a qualified retirement plan.)

Defined Benefit Plan: A type of employee benefit plan in which employees know (through a formula) what they will receive upon retirement or after a specified number of years of employment with an employer. The employer is obligated to contribute funds into the defined benefit plan based on an actuarially determined obligation that takes into consideration the age of the workforce, their length of service and the investment earnings that are projected to be achieved form the funds contributed.

Defined Benefit Plans are over funded if the present value of the future payment obligations to employees is less than the current value of the assets in the Plan. It is under-funded if the obligations exceed the current value of these Plan assets. The Pension Benefit Guaranty Corporation insures a specified amount of these future pension benefit payments on a per employee basis.

Defined Contribution Plan: A type of employee benefit plan in which the employer (Fiduciary) makes annual contributions (usually discretionary in amount or possibly based on a percentage of the profits of the company, e.g., Profit Sharing Plan) into the plan for the ultimate payment to employees at retirement. Each employee's account value will be determined by the contribution made, and the earnings achieved (usually a vesting percentage—20% per year after one year of service).

401(k) Plan: A defined contribution plan that permits employees to have a portion of their salary deducted from their paycheck and contributed to an account. Federal (and sometimes state) taxes on the employee contributions and investment earnings are deferred until the participant receives a distribution from the plan (typically at retirement). Employers may also make contributions to a participant's account.

Department of Labor (DOL): The U.S. Department of Labor (DOL) deals with issues related to the American workforce – including topics concerning pension and benefit plans. Through its branch agency the Pension and Welfare Benefits Administration, the DOL is responsible for administering the provisions of Title I of ERISA.

Disclosure: Plan sponsors must provide plan participants to access to certain types of information, including the summary plan descriptions, summary of material modifications, and summary annual reports.

ERISA: An acronym for Employee Retirement Income Security Act of 1974. "Among its statutes, ERISA calls for proper plan reporting and disclosure to participants."

ESOP (Employee Stock Ownership Plan): A qualified defined contribution plan in which plan assets are invested primarily or exclusively in the securities of the sponsoring employer.

Fiduciary: A person with the authority to make decisions regarding a plan's assets or important administrative matters. Fiduciaries are required under ERISA to make decisions based solely on the best interests of plan participants.

Fiduciary Insurance: Insurance that protects plan fiduciaries in the event that they are found liable for a breach of fiduciary responsibility.

KSOP: A plan arrangement that includes both 401(k) contributions and an ESOP.

Material Modification: A change in the terms of the plan that may affect plan participants, or other changes in a summary plan document (SPD).

Median Market Cap: An indicator of the size of companies in which a fund invests.

Money Market Fund: A mutual fund seeking to generate income for participants through investments in short-term securities.

Money-Purchase Plan: A type of defined contribution plan in which the employer's contributions are determined by a specific formula, usually as a percentage of pay. Contributions are not dependent on company profits.

Multiemployer Plan: A pension plan to which more than one employer contributes, and which is maintained according to collective bargaining agreements.

Mutual Funds: Classes of Fixed Income Funds

A. Money Market Funds - Money market funds are like bank savings accounts in that the value of your investment does not fluctuate. Money market funds, however, are not insured like bank certificates of deposit. The interest rates are generally lower than other forms of fixed income funds.

B. Government Bond Funds - These funds invest in debt from the U.S. government. They are quite conservative, depending on the maturity of the underlying bonds. They generally invest in all types of government bonds, including those backed by the government but not directly issued by the government. Look for bond maturities of five years or less.

C. U.S. Fixed Income - These are funds that invest in all types of U.S. bonds, including government and corporate bonds. They will typically invest in higher-quality investments with little risk of default across a broad range of maturities. Check to see that the credit quality of the bonds is primarily AAA or AA and the average maturities are no longer than five years.

D. High Yield Funds (Junk Bonds) - These funds typically invest in low-quality corporate debt and are subject to high risk of default. They, therefore, tend to offer a higher yield. If safety and stability are important to you, avoid this choice. For similar risk, you could have higher potential returns in equity mutual funds.

E. Global Bond Funds - These funds invest in foreign and U.S. bonds. Historically, global bond funds have outperformed domestic bond funds, but you do assume some additional risk.

F. International Bond Funds - These funds specialize in investing in bonds of foreign governments and companies and are usually riskier than U.S. investments. However, you may realize additional income as compared to U.S. Fixed Income.

Equity Funds: A stock mutual fund is called an equity fund, which is usually a higher-growth vehicle. Obviously, an equity mutual fund, because of its investment risk, is not an appropriate investment for your short-term money or for your intermediate money.

Classes of Equity Funds

1. Growth Mutual Funds - A growth company is one that is doing very well, by any measure. A growth mutual fund is typically defined as one that invests in companies that are exceeding the growth of the economy. Growth companies typically sell at high price/earnings (P/E) ratios, reflecting the expectation that their growth will continue and that the earnings will eventually "catch up" with the high valuations awarded the companies. Growth companies and growth mutual funds can cover all capitalization ranges.

a. Large-Cap Growth - An investment strategy that invests in stocks of large high growth companies with an average capitalization of approximately $7 billion or greater.

b. Mid-Cap Growth - An investment strategy that invests in stocks of mid-sized companies with an average capitalization of between $2 billion and $7 billion.

c. Small-Cap Growth - An investment strategy that invests in stocks of smaller companies with an average capitalization of less than $2 billion.

2. Value Mutual Funds - Value mutual funds invest in companies that are either distressed or relatively under-priced. Value stocks have high book-to-market ratios, which means the stock is trading at a low price compared with its book value. (Book value is defined as the company's assets on a balance sheet, less its liabilities, and is often figured on a per share basis.) In addition, the price/earnings ratio is lower for value stocks, and as such, are generally considered less volatile. As with growth stocks, value stocks can cover all capitalization ranges.

a. Large-Cap Value - An investment strategy that invests in stocks of large companies with an average capitalization of approximately $7 billion or greater.

b. Mid-Cap Value - An investment strategy that invests in stocks of mid-sized companies with an average capitalization of between $2 billion and $7 billion.

c. Small-Cap Value - An investment strategy that invests in stocks of smaller companies with an average capitalization of less than $2 billion.

3. International Equities Funds - The principles of international growth and value are the same as domestic. Growth companies are those that are doing very well. Value companies are those that are either distressed or priced at less than perceived intrinsic value.

a. International Growth - Focus the portfolio on stocks of high-growth international companies.

b. International Value - Focus the portfolio on stocks of undervalued companies worldwide.

Named Fiduciary: The plan document must name one or more fiduciaries, giving them authority to control and manage the operation of the plan. The named fiduciary must also be identified as a fiduciary by a procedure specified in the plan document.

Non-Qualified Deferred Compensation Plan: A plan subject to tax, in which the assets of certain employees (usually Highly Compensated Employees) are deferred. These funds may be reached by an employer's creditors.

Party-In-Interest: Those who are a party-in-interest to a plan include the employer; the directors, officers, employees or owners of the employer; any employee organization whose members are plan participants; plan fiduciaries; and plan service providers.

Pension and Welfare Benefits Administration (PWBA): This branch of the Department of Labor protects the pensions, health plans, and other employee benefits of American workers. The PWBA enforces Title I of ERISA, which contains rules for reporting and disclosure, vesting, participation, funding, and fiduciary conduct.

Pension Benefit Guaranty Corporation (PBGC): A federal agency established by Title IV of ERISA for the insurance of defined benefit pension plans. The PBGC provides payment of pension benefits if a plan terminates and is unable to cover all required benefits.

Plan Administrator: The individual, group or corporation named in the plan document as responsible for day-to-day operations. The plan sponsor is generally the plan administrator if no other entity is named.

Plan Participant: A person who has an account in the plan and any beneficiaries who may be eligible to receive an account balance.

Plan Document: Every 401(k) has a plan document of how your 401(k) operates. The law says so. It is very detailed and contains legal information about your 401(k). In fact, the plan in plan document is why 401(k)s are called 401(k) plans. The law also requires that a summary of the plan document be provided to employees— this is the summary plan description.

Plan Sponsor: The entity responsible for establishing and maintaining the plan.

Plan Year: The calendar, policy, or fiscal year for which plan records are maintained.

Prohibited Transaction: Activities regarding treatment of plan assets by fiduciaries that are prohibited by ERISA. This includes transactions with a party-in-interest including sale, exchange, lease, or loan of plan securities or other properties. Any treatment of plan assets by the fiduciary that is not consistent with the best interests of the plan participants is a prohibited transaction.

Profit Sharing Plan: Company-sponsored plan funded only by company contributions. Company contributions may be determined by a fixed formula related to the employer's profits, or may be at the discretion of the board of directors.

Prudent Investor Rule: Officially named the "Uniform Prudent Investment Act," this standard of prudence was drafted by the National Conference of Commissioners on Uniform State Laws (1994) and has been legislated in a majority of states. Rooted in modern portfolio practices, the Prudent Investor rule emphasizes that an investment portfolio should be examined in its "totality" and that the results of a single investment can only be meaningfully evaluated against this macro framework. This Rule is similar to the Employee Retirement Income and Security Act (ERISA) legislated by Congress in 1974 to safeguard qualified retirement plans.

Qualified Plan: Any plan that qualifies for favorable tax treatment by meeting the requirements of section 401(a) of the Internal Revenue Code and by following applicable regulations. Includes 401(k) and deferred profit sharing plans.

Risk Tolerance: Risk is the variability of returns from an investment and tolerance is leeway for variation from a standard. In other words, your capacity to tolerate unfavorable conditions during the time period you hold your investments.

Service Provider: A company that provides any type of service to the plan, including managing assets, recordkeeping, providing plan education, and administering the plan.

Standard Deviation: Volatility can be statistically measured using standard deviation. Standard deviation describes how far from the mean historic performance has been, either higher or lower. Mean is simply the middle point between the two historic extremes of the performance of the investment you are examining. The standard deviation measurement helps explain what the distribution of returns likely will be. The greater the range of returns, the greater the risk. Generally, the current price of a security reflects the expected total return of its investment and its perceived risk. The lower the risk, the lower the return expected.

Target-Benefit Plan: A type of defined contribution plan in which company contributions are based on an actuarial valuation designed to provide a target benefit to each participant upon retirement. The plan does not guarantee that such benefit will be paid; its only obligation is to pay whatever benefit can be provided by the amount in the participant's account. It is a hybrid of a money-purchase plan and a defined-benefit plan.

Trustee: The individual, bank or trust company having fiduciary responsibility for holding plan assets.

Uniform Prudent Investors Act (UPIA): There are five main points of this law, which removes much of the common law restrictions placed on investment fiduciaries. The following points are directly from the Act.

1. The standard of prudence is applied to any investment as part of the total portfolio, rather than to individual investments. In the trust, setting the term "portfolio" embraces all the trust's assets.

2. The tradeoff in all investing between risk and return is identified as the fiduciary's central consideration.

3. Restrictions on types of investments have been abrogated; the trustee can invest in anything that plays an appropriate role in achieving the risk/return objectives of the trust and that meets the other requirements of prudent investing.

4. The long familiar requirement that fiduciaries diversify their investments has been integrated into the definition of prudent investing.

5. The much-criticized former rule of trust law forbidding the trustee to delegate investment and management functions has been reversed. Delegation is now permitted, subject to safeguards.

Uniform Management of Public Employee Retirement Systems Act (MPERS): This act governs state, county and retirement plans. This Act is very similar to ERISA and the UPIA in that investment decisions must be made for the sole benefit of the participants and beneficiaries of plan assets. Decisions must be made as a prudent man would make with an eye toward controlling all costs associated with the management of the assets.

Appendix 7

RESOURCES

The Center for Fiduciary Studies: www.cfstudies.com
The Center for Fiduciary Studies was established as the first full-time training and research facility focused exclusively on investment fiduciary responsibility and portfolio management.

Donald B. Trone, AIFA™; President of the Foundation for Fiduciary Studies, Director of the Center for Fiduciary Studies, and CEO of Fiduciary Analytics

For additional copies of forms, checklists, and other resources, visit the Thornburgh Investment Management site at *www.thornburginvestmentscom.*

Articles and Treatises

William T. Allen, "Defining the Role of Outside Directors in an Age of Global Competition," Corporate Governance Today and Tomorrow (1992).

Dennis Block, Nancy Barton and Stephen Radin, "The Business Judgment Rule: Fiduciary Duties of Corporate Directors" (4th ed. 1993).

Dennis Block, Michael J. Maimone and Stephen B. Ross, "The Duty of Loyalty and the Evolution of the Scope of Judicial Review," 59 Brooklyn L. Rev. 65 (1993).

Business Roundtable, "Corporate Governance and American Competitiveness," 46 Bus. Law. 241 (1990).

Charles Hansen, "The Duty of Care, the Business Judgment Rule, and the American Law Institute Corporate Governance Project," 48 Bus. Law. 1355 (1993).

Joseph Hinsey, IV, "Business Judgment and the American Law Institute's Corporate Governance Project: The Rule, The Doctrine, and the Reality," 52 Geo. Wash. L. Rev. 609 (1984). Joseph Hinsey, IV, "The Committee System and the Role of Outside Directors," The Evolving Role of Outside Directors (1993).

Fred, Reish, Reish Luftman Reicher & Cohen, Attorneys at Law, 11755 Wilshire Blvd., 10th Floor, Los Angeles, CA 90025-1539 – 310.478.5656 / 310.478.5831 / www.reish.com

Peter Swisher, "Solving an Employer's Fiduciary Dilemma: Liability, Discretion, and the Role of the Qualified Plan Advisor."

"Fiduciary Liability Loss Prevention", Chubb Specialty Insurance.

Jill Elswick, "Scandals Spur Fiduciary Liability Premiums," Employee Benefits News, July 2003.

Jill Elswick, "Caution Advised on Company Stock in Plans," Employee Benefits News, December 2004.

PlanSponsor.com, "Tips on Securing Fiduciary Liability Insurance," Steve Saxon, Groom Law Group.

Mark Larsen, Tillinghast-Towers Perrin, "Fiduciary Liabilities Basics."

Fred Reish, "Taking Stock: The Most Dangerous Investment," February 2005; and "Taking Stock: Managing the Risk of Company Stock," June 2003.

"Fiduciary & Investment Issues: Beyond the Basics," AON, March 2005.

Catherine D. Gordon, "Investment Committees: Vanguard's View of Best Practices."

Greycourt, White Paper No. 31—Reinvigorating the Investment Committee.